quick&easy

essential recipes

Publisher's Note:
Raw or semi-cooked eggs should not be consumed by babies, toddlers, pregnant women,
the elderly or those suffering from recurring illness.

Publisher and Creative Director: Nick Wells
Project Editor: Cat Emslie
Photographers: Paul Forrester, Colin Bowling and Stephen Brayne
Home Economists & Stylists: Jaqueline Bellefontaine, Mandy Phipps,
Vicki Smallwood and Penny Stephens
Art Director: Mike Spender
Layout Design: Dave Jones
Digital Design and Production: Chris Herbert
Editorial Assistant: Chelsea Edwards
Proofreader: Dawn Laker

10 12 11

5 7 9 10 8 6 4

This edition first published 2008 by
FLAME TREE PUBLISHING
Crabtree Hall, Crabtree Lane
Fulham, London SW6 6TY
United Kingdom

www.flametreepublishing.com

Flame Tree is part of the Foundry Creative Media Co. Ltd
© 2008 The Foundry Creative Media Co. Ltd

ISBN 978-1-84786-999-9

A CIP Record for this book is available from the British Library upon request

Printed in China

quick&easy

essential recipes

General Editor: Gina Steer

**FLAME TREE
PUBLISHING**

Contents

Effortless Desserts. 112

Entertaining. 148

Useful Conversions

Liquid Measures
Metric/Imperial

2.5 ml . . . . ½ teaspoon	200 ml . . . . 7 fl oz (⅓ pint)	1 litre . . . . 1¾ pints
5 ml . . . . 1 teaspoon	250 ml . . . . 8 fl oz	1.1 litres . . . . 2 pints
15 ml . . . . 1 tablespoon	275 ml . . . . 9 fl oz	1.25 litres . . . . . 2¼ pints
25 ml . . . . 1 fl oz	300 ml . . . . ½ pint (10 fl oz)	1.5 litres . . . . 2½ pints
50 ml . . . . 2 fl oz	350 ml . . . . 12 fl oz	1.6 litres . . . . 2¾ pints
65 ml . . . . 2½ fl oz	400 ml . . . . 14 fl oz	1.7 litres . . . . 3 pints
85 ml . . . . 3 fl oz	450 ml . . . . ¾ pint (15 fl oz)	2 litres . . . . 3½ pints
100 ml . . . . 3½ fl oz	475 ml . . . . 16 fl oz	2.25 litres . . . . . 4 pints
120 ml . . . . 4 fl oz	500 ml . . . . 18 fl oz	2.5 litres . . . . 4½ pints
135 ml . . . . 4½ fl oz	600 ml . . . . 1 pint (20 fl oz)	2.75 litres . . . . . 5 pints
150 ml . . . . ¼ pint (5 fl oz)	750 ml . . . . 1¼ pints	
175 ml . . . . 6 fl oz	900 ml . . . . 1½ pints	

Oven Temperatures

110°C	225°F	Gas Mark ¼	Very slow oven
120/130°C	250°F	Gas Mark ½	Very slow oven
140°C	275°F	Gas Mark 1	Slow oven
150°C	300°F	Gas Mark 2	Slow oven
160/170°C	325°F	Gas Mark 3	Moderate oven
180°C	350°F	Gas Mark 4	Moderate oven
190°C	375°F	Gas Mark 5	Moderately hot oven
200°C	400°F	Gas Mark 6	Moderately hot oven
220°C	425°F	Gas Mark 7	Hot oven
230°C	450°F	Gas Mark 8	Hot oven
240°C	475°F	Gas Mark 9	Very hot oven

Dry Weights
Metric/Imperial

10 g	¼ oz	165 g	5½ oz	450 g	1 lb (16 oz)
15 g	½ oz	175 g	6 oz		
20 g	¾ oz	185 g	6½ oz		
25 g	1 oz	200 g	7 oz		
40 g	1½ oz	225 g	8 oz		
50 g	2 oz	250 g	9 oz		
65 g	2½ oz	300 g	10 oz		
75 g	3 oz	325 g	11 oz		
90 g	3½ oz	350 g	12 oz		
100 g	4 oz	375 g	13 oz		
120 g	4½ oz	400 g	14 oz		
150 g	5 oz	425 g	15 oz		

Temperature Conversion

−4°F	−20°C	95°F	35°C
5°F	−15°C	104°F	40°C
14°F	−10°C	113°F	45°C
23°F	−5°C	122°F	50°C
32°F	0°C	212°F	100°C
41°F	5°C		
50°F	10°C		
59°F	15°C		
68°F	20°C		
77°F	25°C		
86°F	30°C		

Good Cooking Rules

When handling and cooking foods, there are a few rules and guidelines that should be observed so that food remains fit to eat and uncontaminated with the bacteria and bugs that can result in food poisoning.

Good Hygiene Rules

- Personal hygiene is imperative when handling food. Before commencing, wash hands thoroughly with soap, taking particular care with nails. Always wash hands after going to the toilet. Wash again after handling raw foods, cooked meats or vegetables. Do not touch any part of the body or handle pets, rubbish or dirty washing during food preparation.
- Cuts should be covered with a waterproof plaster, preferably blue so it can be easily seen if lost.
- Do not smoke in the kitchen.
- Keep pets off all work surfaces and out of the kitchen if possible. Clean surfaces with an anti-bacterial solution. Wash their eating bowls separately.
- Ensure that hair is off the face and does not trail into food or machinery.
- Use a dishwasher wherever possible and wash utensils and equipment in very hot, soapy water.
- Use clean dish cloths and tea towels, replacing regularly or boiling them to kill any bacteria.

- Chopping boards and cooking implements must be clean. Boards should either be washed in a dishwasher or scrubbed after each use. Keep a separate board for meat, fish and vegetables and wash knives before using on different types of food. Use separate boards for raw and cooked food or wash them thoroughly in-between.
- Use dustbin liners for rubbish and empty regularly, cleaning your bin with disinfectant. Dustbins should be outside.

Guidelines for Using a Refrigerator

- Ensure that the refrigerator is situated away from any equipment that gives off heat, such as the cooker, washing machine or tumble drier, to ensures the greatest efficiency. Ensure that the vents are not obstructed.
- If not frost-free, defrost regularly, wiping down with a mild solution of bicarbonate of soda dissolved in warm water and a clean cloth.
- Close the door as quickly as possible so that the motor does not have to work overtime to keep it at the correct temperature.
- Ensure that the temperature is 5°C. A thermometer is a good investment.
- Avoid over-loading – this just makes the motor work harder.
- Cool food before placing in the refrigerator and always cover to avoid any smells or transference of taste to other foods.

Stacking Your Refrigerator

- Remove supermarket packaging from raw meat, poultry and fish, place on a plate or dish, cover loosely and store at the base of the refrigerator to ensure that the juices do not drip on other foods.

- Store cheese in a box or container, wrapped to prevent the cheese drying out.
- Remove food to be eaten raw 30 minutes before use so it can return to room temperature.
- Cooked meats, bacon and all cooked dishes should be stored at the top – this is the coldest part.
- Store eggs in the egg compartment and remove 30 minutes before cooking in order to return them to temperature.
- Butter and all fats can be stored on the door, as can milk, cold drinks, sauces, mayonnaise and preserves with low sugar content.
- Cream and other dairy products, as well as pastries such as chocolate éclairs, should be stored on the middle shelf.
- Vegetables, salad and fruit should be stored in the salad boxes at the bottom of the refrigerator.
- Soft fruits should be kept in the salad box along with mushrooms, which are best kept in paper bags.
- To avoid cross-contamination, raw and cooked foods must be stored separately.
- Use all foods by the sell-by date – once opened, treat as cooked foods and use within two days.

General Rules

- Use all foods by the use-by date and store correctly. This applies to all foods: fresh, frozen, canned and dried. Potatoes are best if removed from polythene, stored in brown paper and kept in the cool and dark.

- Ensure that all food is thoroughly thawed before use, unless meant to be cooked from frozen.
- Cook all poultry thoroughly at the correct temperature (190°C/375°F/Gas Mark 5) ensuring that the juices run clear.
- Leave foods to cool as quickly as possible before placing in the refrigerator, and cover while cooling.
- Do not re-freeze any thawed frozen foods unless cooked first.
- Date and label frozen food and use in rotation.
- Re-heat foods thoroughly until piping hot. Remember to allow foods to stand when using the microwave and stir to distribute the heat.
- Microwaves vary according to make and wattage – always refer to manufacturer's instructions.
- Only re-heat dishes once and always heat until piping hot.
- Ensure that eggs are fresh. If using for mayonnaise, soufflés or other dishes that use raw or semi-cooked egg, do not give to the vulnerable – the elderly, pregnant women, those with a recurring illness, toddlers and babies.
- When buying frozen foods, transport in freezer-insulated bags, placing in the freezer as soon as possible after purchase.
- Chilled foods, such as cold meats, cheese, fresh meat, fish and dairy products should be bought, taken home and placed in the refrigerator immediately. Do not keep in a warm car or room.
- Avoid buying damaged or unlabelled canned goods. Keep store cupboards clean, wiping down regularly and rotating the food.
- Flour, nuts, rice, pulses, grains and pasta should be checked regularly and once opened, placed in airtight containers.
- Do not buy eggs or frozen or chilled foods that are damaged in any way.
- Keep dried herbs and ready-ground spices in a cool, dark place. They quickly lose their pungency and flavour when exposed to light.

Simple Soups & Easy Starters

Whether you want to make a comforting home-cooked soup or a light and tasty snack, these starters could not be more simple with their easy to follow, step-by-step instructions and pictures to guide you along.

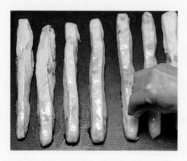

Cream of Spinach Soup

1 Place the onion, garlic and potatoes in a large saucepan and cover with the cold water. Add half the salt and bring to the boil. Cover and simmer for 15–20 minutes, or until the potatoes are tender. Remove from the heat and add the spinach. Cover and set aside for 10 minutes.

2 Slowly melt the butter in another saucepan, add the flour and cook over a low heat for about 2 minutes. Remove the saucepan from the heat and add the milk, a little at a time, stirring continuously. Return to the heat and cook, stirring continuously for 5–8 minutes, or until the sauce is smooth and slightly thickened. Add the freshly grated nutmeg, or to taste.

3 Blend the cooled potato and spinach mixture in a food processor or blender to a smooth purée, then return to the saucepan and gradually stir in the white sauce. Season to taste with salt and pepper and gently reheat, taking care not to allow the soup to boil. Ladle into soup bowls and top with spoonfuls of crème fraîche or soured cream. Serve immediately with warm focaccia bread.

Ingredients   SERVES 6–8

1 large onion, peeled and chopped
5 large plump garlic cloves,
    peeled and chopped
2 medium potatoes,
    peeled and chopped
750 ml/1¼ pints cold water
1 tsp salt
450 g/1 lb spinach, washed and
    large stems removed
50 g/2 oz butter
3 tbsp flour
750 ml/1¼ pints milk
½ tsp freshly grated nutmeg
freshly ground black pepper
6–8 tbsp crème fraîche or
    soured cream
warm focaccia bread, to serve

Helpful hint

When choosing spinach, always look for fresh, crisp, dark green leaves. Use within 1–2 days of buying and store in a cool place until needed.

Rich Tomato Soup with Roasted Red Peppers

1 Preheat the oven to 200°C/400°F/Gas Mark 6. Lightly oil a roasting tin with 1 teaspoon of the olive oil. Place the peppers and tomatoes cut-side down in the roasting tin with the onion quarters and the garlic cloves. Spoon over the remaining oil.

2 Bake in the preheated oven for 30 minutes, or until the skins on the peppers have started to blacken and blister. Allow the vegetables to cool for about 10 minutes, then remove the skins, stalks and seeds from the peppers. Peel away the skins from the tomatoes and onions and squeeze out the garlic.

3 Place the cooked vegetables into a blender or food processor and blend until smooth. Add the stock and blend again to form a smooth purée. Pour the puréed soup through a sieve, if a smooth soup is preferred, then pour into a saucepan. Bring to the boil, simmer gently for 2–3 minutes and season to taste with salt and pepper. Serve hot with a swirl of soured cream and a sprinkling of shredded basil on the top.

Ingredients   SERVES 4

2 tsp light olive oil
700 g/1¹/₂ lb red peppers, halved and deseeded
450 g/1 lb ripe plum tomatoes, halved
2 onions, unpeeled and quartered
4 garlic cloves, unpeeled
600 ml/1 pint chicken stock
salt and freshly ground black pepper
4 tbsp soured cream
1 tbsp freshly shredded basil

Helpful hint

To help remove the skins of the peppers more easily, remove them from the oven and put immediately into a plastic bag or a bowl covered with clingfilm. Leave until cool enough to handle then skin carefully.

Cream of Pumpkin Soup

1 Cut the skinned and de-seeded pumpkin flesh into 2.5 cm/1 inch cubes. Heat the olive oil in a large saucepan and cook the pumpkin for 2–3 minutes, coating it completely with oil. Chop the onion and leek finely and cut the carrot and celery into small dice.

2 Add the vegetables to the saucepan with the garlic and cook, stirring, for 5 minutes or until they have begun to soften. Cover the vegetables with the water and bring to the boil. Season with plenty of salt and pepper and the nutmeg, cover and simmer for 15–20 minutes, or until all of the vegetables are tender.

3 When the vegetables are tender, remove from the heat, cool slightly then pour into a food processor or blender. Liquidise to form a smooth purée then pass through a sieve into a clean saucepan.

4 Adjust the seasoning to taste and add all but 2 tablespoons of the cream and enough water to obtain the correct consistency. Bring the soup to boiling point, add the cayenne pepper and serve immediately swirled with cream and warm herby bread.

Ingredients   SERVES 4

900 g/2 lb pumpkin flesh (after peeling and discarding the seeds)
4 tbsp olive oil
1 large onion, peeled
1 leek, trimmed
1 carrot, peeled
2 celery sticks
4 garlic cloves, peeled and crushed
1.7 litres/3 pints water
salt and freshly ground black pepper
$^1/_4$ tsp freshly grated nutmeg
150 ml/$^1/_4$ pint single cream
$^1/_4$ tsp cayenne pepper
warm herby bread, to serve

Tasty tip

If you cannot find pumpkin, try replacing it with squash. Butternut, acorn or turban squash would all make suitable substitutes. Avoid spaghetti squash which is not firm-fleshed when cooked.

Peperonata (Braised Mixed Peppers)

1 Remove the seeds from the peppers and cut into thin strips. Slice the onion into rings and chop the garlic cloves finely.

2 Heat the olive oil in a frying pan and fry the peppers, onions and garlic for 5–10 minutes, or until soft and lightly coloured. Stir continuously.

3 Make a cross on the top of the tomatoes then place in a bowl and cover with boiling water. Allow to stand for about 2 minutes. Drain, then remove the skins and seeds and chop the tomato flesh into cubes.

4 Add the tomatoes and oregano to the peppers and onion and season to taste with salt and pepper. Cover the pan and bring to the boil. Simmer gently for about 30 minutes, or until tender, adding the chicken or vegetable stock halfway through the cooking time.

5 Garnish with sprigs of oregano and serve hot with plenty of freshly baked focaccia bread or alternatively lightly toast slices of flatbread and pile a spoonful of peperonata on to each plate.

Ingredients   SERVES 4

2 green peppers
1 red pepper
1 yellow pepper
1 orange pepper
1 onion, peeled
2 garlic cloves, peeled
2 tbsp olive oil
4 very ripe tomatoes
1 tbsp freshly chopped oregano
salt and freshly ground black pepper
150 ml/^{1}/$_4$ pint light chicken or
    vegetable stock
sprigs of fresh oregano, to garnish
focaccia or flatbread, to serve

Tasty tip

Serve the peperonata cold as part of an antipasti platter. Some good accompaniments would be marinated olives, sun-dried or semi-dried marinated tomatoes, sliced salamis and other cold meats and plenty of Italian bread.

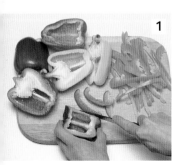

1

2

4

Wild Garlic Mushrooms with Pizza Breadsticks

1 Preheat the oven to 240°C/475°F/Gas Mark 9, 15 minutes before baking. Place the dried yeast in the warm water for 10 minutes. Place the flour in a large bowl and gradually blend in the olive oil, salt and the dissolved yeast.

2 Knead on a lightly floured surface to form a smooth and pliable dough. Cover with clingfilm and leave in a warm place for 15 minutes to allow the dough to rise, then roll out again and cut into sticks of equal length. Cover and leave to rise again for 10 minutes. Brush with the olive oil, sprinkle with salt and bake in the preheated oven for 10 minutes.

3 Pour 3 tablespoons of the oil into a frying pan and add the crushed garlic. Cook over a very low heat, stirring well, for 3–4 minutes to flavour the oil.

4 Cut the wild mushrooms into bite-size slices if very large, then add to the pan. Season well with salt and pepper and cook very gently for 6–8 minutes, or until tender.

5 Whisk the fresh herbs, the remaining olive oil and lemon juice together. Pour over the mushrooms and heat through. Season to taste and place on individual serving dishes. Serve with the pizza breadsticks.

Ingredients   SERVES 6

For the breadsticks:
7 g/¹⁄₄ oz dried yeast
250 ml/8 fl oz warm water
400 g/14 oz strong plain flour
2 tbsp olive oil
1 tsp salt

For the mushrooms:
9 tbsp olive oil
4 garlic cloves, peeled and crushed
450 g/1 lb mixed wild mushrooms, wiped and dried
salt and freshly ground black pepper
1 tbsp freshly chopped parsley
1 tbsp freshly chopped basil
1 tsp fresh oregano leaves
juice of 1 lemon

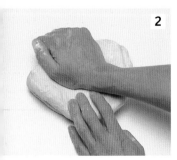
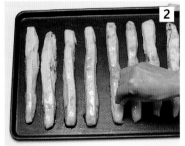

Hot Tiger Prawns with Parma Ham

1 Preheat the oven to 180°C/350°F/Gas Mark 4. Slice the cucumber and tomatoes thinly, then arrange on four large plates and reserve. Peel the prawns, leaving the tail shell intact and remove the thin black vein running down the back.

2 Whisk together 4 tablespoons of the olive oil, garlic and chopped parsley in a small bowl and season to taste with plenty of salt and pepper. Add the prawns to the mixture and stir until they are well coated. Remove the prawns, then wrap each one in a piece of Parma ham and secure with a cocktail stick.

3 Place the prepared prawns on a lightly oiled baking sheet or dish with the slices of bread and cook in the preheated oven for 5 minutes.

4 Remove the prawns from the oven and spoon the wine over the prawns and bread. Return to the oven and cook for a further 10 minutes until piping hot.

5 Carefully remove the cocktail sticks and arrange three prawn rolls on each slice of bread. Place on top of the sliced cucumber and tomatoes and serve immediately.

Ingredients   SERVES 4

½ cucumber, peeled if preferred

4 ripe tomatoes

12 raw tiger prawns

6 tbsp olive oil

4 garlic cloves, peeled and crushed

4 tbsp freshly chopped parsley

salt and freshly ground black pepper

6 slices of Parma ham, cut in half

4 slices Italian flatbread

4 tbsp dry white wine

Helpful hint

The black intestinal vein needs to be removed from raw prawns because it can cause a bitter flavour. Remove the shell then, using a small, sharp knife, make a cut along the centre back of the prawn and open out the flesh. Using the tip of the knife, remove the thread that lies along the length of the prawn and discard.

Mozzarella Parcels with Cranberry Relish

1 Slice the mozzarella thinly, remove the crusts from the bread and make sandwiches with the bread and cheese. Cut into 5 cm/2 inch squares and squash them quite flat. Season the eggs with salt and pepper, then soak the bread in the seasoned egg for 1 minute on each side until well coated.

2 Heat the oil to 190°C/375°F and deep-fry the bread squares for 1–2 minutes, or until they are crisp and golden brown. Drain on absorbent kitchen paper and keep warm while the cranberry relish is prepared.

3 Place the cranberries, orange juice, rind, sugar and port into a small saucepan and add 5 tablespoons of water. Bring to the boil, then simmer for 10 minutes, or until the cranberries have 'popped'. Sweeten with a little more sugar if necessary.

4 Arrange the mozzarella parcels on individual serving plates. Serve with a little of the cranberry relish.

Ingredients   SERVES 6
125 g/4 oz mozzarella cheese
8 slices thin white bread
2 medium eggs, beaten
salt and freshly ground black pepper
300 ml/¹/₂ pint olive oil

For the relish:
125 g/4 oz cranberries
2 tbsp fresh orange juice
grated rind of 1 small orange
50 g/2 oz soft light brown sugar
1 tbsp port

Helpful hint
Frying in oil that is not hot enough causes food to absorb more oil than it would if fried at the correct temperature. To test the temperature of the oil without a thermometer, drop a cube of bread into the frying pan. If the bread browns in 30 seconds the oil is at the right temperature.

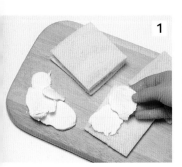
1

1

3

Beetroot Ravioli with Dill Cream Sauce

1 Heat the olive oil in a large frying pan, add the onion and caraway seeds and cook over a medium heat for 5 minutes, or until the onion is softened and lightly golden. Stir in the beetroot and cook for 5 minutes. Blend the beetroot mixture in a food processor until smooth, then allow to cool. Stir in the ricotta cheese, breadcrumbs, egg yolk and Parmesan cheese. Season the filling to taste with salt and pepper and reserve.

2 Divide the pasta dough into eight pieces. Roll out as for tagliatelle, but do not cut the sheets in half. Lay 1 sheet on a floured surface and place 5 heaped teaspoons of the filling 2.5 cm/1 inch apart.

3 Dampen around the heaps of filling and lay a second sheet of pasta over the top. Press around the heaps to seal. Cut into squares using a pastry wheel or sharp knife. Put the filled pasta shapes on to a floured tea towel. Bring a large pan of lightly salted water to a rolling boil. Drop the ravioli into the boiling water, return to the boil and cook for 3–4 minutes until 'al dente'.

4 Meanwhile, heat the walnut oil in a small pan then add the chopped dill and green peppercorns. Remove from the heat, stir in the crème fraîche and season well. Drain the cooked pasta thoroughly and toss with the sauce. Tip into warmed serving dishes and serve immediately.

Ingredients   SERVES 4–6

bought fresh pasta dough

1 tbsp olive oil

1 small onion, peeled and
   finely chopped

$1/_2$ tsp caraway seeds

175 g/6 oz cooked beetroot, chopped

175 g/6 oz ricotta cheese

25 g/1 oz fresh white breadcrumbs

1 medium egg yolk

2 tbsp grated Parmesan cheese

salt and freshly ground black pepper

4 tbsp walnut oil

4 tbsp freshly chopped dill

1 tbsp green peppercorns,
   drained and roughly chopped

6 tbsp crème fraîche

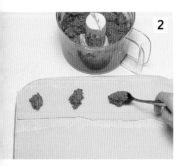

Gnocchi with Grilled Cherry Tomato Sauce

1   Preheat the grill just before required. Bring a large pan of
    salted water to the boil, add the potatoes and cook for
    20–25 minutes until tender. Drain. Leave until cool enough to
    handle but still hot, then peel them and place in a large bowl.
    Mash until smooth then work in the egg, salt and enough of
    the flour to form a soft dough.

2   With floured hands, roll a spoonful of the dough into a small
    ball. Flatten the ball slightly on to the back of a large fork,
    then roll it off the fork to make a little ridged dumpling. Place
    each gnocchi on to a floured tea towel as you work.

3   Place the tomatoes in a flameproof shallow dish. Add the
    garlic, lemon zest, herbs and olive oil. Season to taste with
    salt and pepper and sprinkle over the sugar. Cook under the
    preheated grill for 10 minutes, or until the tomatoes are
    charred and tender, stirring once or twice.

4   Meanwhile, bring a large pan of lightly salted water to the
    boil, then reduce to a steady simmer. Dropping in 6–8
    gnocchi at a time, cook in batches for 3–4 minutes, or until
    they begin bobbing up to the surface. Remove with a slotted
    spoon and drain well on absorbent kitchen paper before
    transferring to a warmed serving dish; cover with foil. Toss
    the cooked gnocchi with the tomato sauce. Serve
    immediately with a little grated Parmesan cheese.

Ingredients   SERVES 4

450 g/1 lb floury potatoes, unpeeled
1 medium egg
1 tsp salt
75–90 g/3–3$^1/_2$ oz plain flour
450 g/1 lb mixed red and
    orange cherry tomatoes,
    halved lengthways
2 garlic cloves, peeled and
    finely sliced
zest of $^1/_2$ lemon, finely grated
1 tbsp freshly chopped thyme
1 tbsp freshly chopped basil
2 tbsp extra virgin olive oil, plus extra
    for drizzling
salt and freshly ground black pepper
pinch of sugar
freshly grated Parmesan cheese,
    to serve

Helpful hint

When cooking the gnocchi, use a very
large pan with at least 1.7 litres/3 pints
of water to give them plenty of room
so that they do not stick together.

Tiny Pasta with Fresh Herb Sauce

1   Bring a large pan of lightly salted water to a rolling boil. Add the pasta and cook according to the packet instructions, or until 'al dente'.

2   Meanwhile, place all the herbs, the lemon zest, olive oil, garlic and chilli flakes in a heavy-based pan. Heat gently for 2–3 minutes, or until the herbs turn bright green and become very fragrant. Remove from the heat and season to taste with salt and pepper.

3   Drain the pasta thoroughly, reserving 2–3 tablespoons of the cooking water. Transfer the pasta to a large warmed bowl.

4   Pour the heated herb mixture over the pasta and toss together until thoroughly mixed. Check and adjust the seasoning, adding a little of the pasta cooking water if the pasta mixture seems a bit dry. Transfer to warmed serving dishes and serve immediately with grated Parmesan cheese.

Ingredients   SERVES 6

375 g/13 oz tripolini
   (small bows with rounded ends)
   or small farfalle
2 tbsp freshly chopped flat-
   leaf parsley
2 tbsp freshly chopped basil
1 tbsp freshly snipped chives
1 tbsp freshly chopped chervil
1 tbsp freshly chopped tarragon
1 tbsp freshly chopped sage
1 tbsp freshly chopped oregano
1 tbsp freshly chopped marjoram
1 tbsp freshly chopped thyme
1 tbsp freshly chopped rosemary
finely grated zest of 1 lemon
75 ml/3 fl oz extra virgin olive oil
2 garlic cloves, peeled and
   finely chopped
$\frac{1}{2}$ tsp dried chilli flakes
salt and freshly ground black pepper
freshly grated Parmesan cheese,
   to serve

Louisiana Prawns & Fettuccine

1   Heat 2 tablespoons of the olive oil in a large saucepan and add the reserved prawn shells and heads. Fry over a high heat for 2–3 minutes, until the shells turn pink and are lightly browned. Add half the shallots, half the garlic, half the basil and the carrot, onion, celery, parsley and thyme. Season lightly with salt, pepper and cayenne and sauté for 2–3 minutes, stirring often. Pour in the wine and stir, scraping the pan well. Bring to the boil and simmer for 1 minute, then add the tomatoes. Cook for a further 3–4 minutes then pour in 200 ml/7 fl oz water. Bring to the boil, lower the heat and simmer for about 30 minutes, stirring often and using a wooden spoon to mash the prawn shells in order to release as much flavour as possible into the sauce. Lower the heat if the sauce is reducing very quickly. Strain through a sieve, pressing well to extract as much liquid as possible; there should be about 450 ml/³/₄ pint. Pour the liquid into a clean pan and bring to the boil, then lower the heat and simmer gently until the liquid is reduced by about half.

2   Heat the remaining oil over a high heat in a frying pan and add the peeled prawns. Season lightly and add the lemon juice. Cook for 1 minute, lower the heat and add the remaining shallots and garlic. Cook for 1 minute. Add the sauce and adjust the seasoning. Meanwhile, bring a large pan of lightly salted water to a rolling boil and add the fettuccine. Once cooked, drain thoroughly. Transfer to a warmed serving dish. Add the sauce and toss well. Garnish with the remaining basil and serve immediately.

Ingredients   SERVES 4

4 tbsp olive oil
450 g/1 lb raw tiger prawns,
  washed and peeled, shells and
  heads reserved
2 shallots, peeled and finely chopped
4 garlic cloves, peeled and
  finely chopped
large handful fresh basil leaves
1 carrot, peeled and finely chopped
1 onion, peeled and finely chopped
1 celery stick, trimmed and
  finely chopped
2–3 sprigs fresh parsley
2–3 sprigs fresh thyme
salt and freshly ground black pepper
pinch cayenne pepper
175 ml/6 fl oz dry white wine
450 g/1 lb ripe tomatoes,
  roughly chopped
juice of ¹/₂ lemon, or to taste
350 g/12 oz fettuccine

Gnocchetti with Broccoli & Bacon Sauce

1 Bring a large pan of salted water to the boil. Add the broccoli florets and cook for about 8–10 minutes, or until very soft. Drain thoroughly, allow to cool slightly then chop finely and reserve.

2 Heat the olive oil in a heavy-based pan, add the pancetta or bacon and cook over a medium heat for 5 minutes, or until golden and crisp. Add the onion and cook for a further 5 minutes, or until soft and lightly golden. Add the garlic and cook for 1 minute.

3 Transfer the chopped broccoli to the bacon or pancetta mixture and pour in the milk. Bring slowly to the boil and simmer rapidly for about 15 minutes, or until reduced to a creamy texture.

4 Meanwhile, bring a large pan of lightly salted water to a rolling boil. Add the pasta and cook according to the packet instructions, or until 'al dente'.

5 Drain the pasta thoroughly, reserving a little of the cooking water. Add the pasta and the Parmesan cheese to the broccoli mixture. Toss, adding enough of the reserved cooking water to make a creamy sauce. Season to taste with salt and pepper. Serve immediately with extra Parmesan cheese.

Ingredients   SERVES 6

450 g/1 lb broccoli florets
4 tbsp olive oil
50 g/2 oz pancetta or smoked
   bacon, finely chopped
1 small onion, peeled and
   finely chopped
3 garlic cloves, peeled and sliced
200 ml/7 fl oz milk
450 g/1 lb gnocchetti (little
   elongated ribbed shells)
50 g/2 oz freshly grated Parmesan
   cheese, plus extra to serve
salt and freshly ground black pepper

Food fact

Pancetta is an Italian streaky bacon that may be either smoked or unsmoked. You can buy it sliced or in a piece, but it is often sold pre-packed, cut into tiny cubes ready for cooking. Thickly cut, rindless smoked streaky bacon makes a good alternative.

Spicy Chicken with Open Ravioli & Tomato Sauce

1 Heat the olive oil in a frying pan, add the onion and cook gently for 2–3 minutes then add the cumin, paprika and cinnamon and cook for a further 1 minute. Add the chicken, season to taste with salt and pepper and cook for 3–4 minutes, or until tender. Add the peanut butter and stir until well mixed and reserve.

2 Melt the butter in the frying pan, add the shallot and cook for 2 minutes. Add the tomatoes and garlic and season to taste. Simmer gently for 20 minutes, or until thickened, then keep the sauce warm.

3 Cut each sheet of lasagne into six squares. Bring a large pan of lightly salted water to a rolling boil. Add the lasagne squares and cook according to the packet instructions, for about 3–4 minutes, or until 'al dente'. Drain the lasagne pieces thoroughly, reserve and keep warm.

4 Layer the pasta squares with the spicy filling on individual warmed plates. Pour over a little of the hot tomato sauce and sprinkle with chopped coriander. Serve immediately.

Ingredients   SERVES 2–3

2 tbsp olive oil
1 onion, peeled and finely chopped
1 tsp ground cumin
1 tsp hot paprika
1 tsp ground cinnamon
175 g/6 oz boneless and skinless
    chicken breasts, chopped
salt and freshly ground black pepper
1 tbsp smooth peanut butter
50 g/2 oz butter
1 shallot, peeled and finely chopped
2 garlic cloves, peeled and crushed
400 g can chopped tomatoes
125 g/4 oz fresh egg lasagne
2 tbsp freshly chopped coriander

Helpful hint

Remember that fresh pasta should be exactly that; buy no more than two days ahead and preferably on the day that you plan to cook it. Because it contains fresh eggs it should always be stored in the refrigerator.

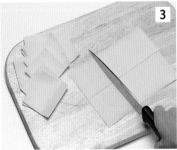

Conchiglioni with Crab au Gratin

1. Preheat the oven to 200°C/400°F/Gas Mark 6, 15 minutes before cooking. Bring a large pan of lightly salted water to a rolling boil. Add the pasta shells and cook according to the packet instructions, or until 'al dente'. Drain thoroughly and allow to dry completely.

2. Melt half the butter in a heavy-based pan, add the shallots and chilli and cook for 2 minutes, then stir in the crab meat. Stuff the cooled shells with the crab mixture and reserve.

3. Melt the remaining butter in a small pan and stir in the flour. Cook for 1 minute, then whisk in the wine and milk and cook, stirring, until thickened. Stir in the crème fraîche and grated cheese and season the sauce to taste with salt and pepper.

4. Place the crab-filled shells in a lightly oiled, large shallow baking dish or tray and spoon over a little of the sauce. Toss the breadcrumbs in the melted butter or oil, then sprinkle over the pasta shells. Bake in the preheated oven for 10 minutes. Serve immediately with a cheese or tomato sauce and a tossed green salad or cooked baby vegetables.

Ingredients   SERVES 4

175 g/6 oz large pasta shells
50 g/2 oz butter
1 shallot, peeled and finely chopped
1 bird's-eye chilli, deseeded and
    finely chopped
2 x 200 g cans crabmeat, drained
3 tbsp plain flour
50 ml/2 fl oz white wine
50 ml/2 fl oz milk
3 tbsp crème fraîche
15 g/¹/₂ oz Cheddar cheese, grated
salt and freshly ground black pepper
1 tbsp oil or melted butter
50 g/2 oz fresh white breadcrumbs

To serve:

cheese, or tomato, sauce
tossed green salad or freshly cooked
    baby vegetables

Pasta Triangles with Pesto & Walnut Dressing

1 Preheat the grill to high. Cut the lasagne sheets in half, then into triangles and reserve. Mix the pesto and ricotta cheese together and warm gently in a pan.

2 Toast the walnuts under the preheated grill until golden. Rub off the papery skins. Place the nuts in a food processor with the bread and grind finely.

3 Mix the soured cream with the mascarpone cheese in a bowl. Add the ground walnuts and grated pecorino cheese and season to taste with salt and pepper. Whisk in the olive oil. Pour into a pan and warm gently.

4 Bring a large pan of lightly salted water to a rolling boil. Add the pasta triangles and cook according to the packet instructions, for about 3–4 minutes, or until 'al dente'.

5 Drain the pasta thoroughly and arrange a few triangles on each serving plate. Top each one with a spoonful of the pesto mixture then place another triangle on top. Continue to layer the pasta and pesto mixture, then spoon a little of the walnut sauce on top of each stack. Garnish with dill, basil or parsley and serve immediately with a freshly dressed tomato and cucumber salad.

Ingredients   SERVES 6

450 g/1 lb fresh egg lasagne
4 tbsp ricotta cheese
4 tbsp pesto
125 g/4 oz walnuts
1 slice white bread, crusts removed
150 ml/¼ pint soured cream
75 g/3 oz mascarpone cheese
25 g/1 oz pecorino cheese, grated
salt and freshly ground black pepper
1 tbsp olive oil
sprig of dill or freshly chopped
    basil or parsley, to garnish
tomato and cucumber salad, to serve

Tasty tip

For a simple tomato and cucumber salad, arrange overlapping thin slices of cucumber and plum tomatoes on a large plate. Drizzle over a dressing made with 1 tsp Dijon mustard, 4 tbsp extra virgin olive oil, 1 tbsp lemon juice and a pinch each of caster sugar, salt and pepper.

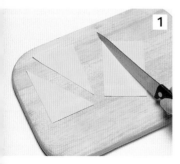

Hassle-free Main Courses

Packed with straightforward recipes, this section gives a range of meals that are approachable enough for beginners. If you are planning to cook for others you need not worry about catering for different tastes, this section caters for everyone, with healthy fish dishes, meat dishes for meat lovers and vegetarian alternatives.

Fruits de Mer Stir-fry

1 Prepare the shellfish. Peel the prawns and, if necessary, remove the thin black veins from the backs of the prawns. Lightly rinse the squid rings and clean the scallops, if necessary.

2 Remove and discard any mussels that are open. Scrub and de-beard the remaining mussels, removing any barnacles from the shells. Cover the mussels with cold water until required.

3 Peel the root ginger and either grate coarsely or shred finely with a sharp knife and place into a small bowl.

4 Add the garlic and chillies to the small bowl, pour in the soy sauce and mix well.

5 Place the mixed shellfish, except the mussels, in a bowl and pour over the marinade. Stir, cover and leave for 15 minutes.

6 Heat a wok until hot, then add the oil and heat until almost smoking. Add the prepared vegetables, stir-fry for 3 minutes, then stir in the plum sauce.

7 Add the shellfish and the mussels with the marinade and stir-fry for a further 3–4 minutes, or until the fish is cooked. Discard any mussels that have not opened. Garnish with the spring onions and serve immediately with the freshly cooked rice.

Ingredients SERVES 4

450 g/1 lb mixed fresh shellfish, such as tiger prawns, squid, scallops and mussels
2.5 cm/1 inch piece fresh root ginger
2 garlic cloves, peeled and crushed
2 green chillies, deseeded and finely chopped
3 tbsp light soy sauce
2 tbsp olive oil
200 g/7 oz baby sweetcorn, rinsed
200 g/7 oz asparagus tips, trimmed and cut in half
200 g/7 oz mangetout, trimmed
2 tbsp plum sauce
4 spring onions, trimmed and shredded, to garnish
freshly cooked rice, to serve

Helpful hint

When stir-frying, it is important that the wok is heated before the oil is added. This ensures that the food does not stick to the wok.

Sardines with Redcurrants

1 Preheat the grill and line the grill rack with foil 2–3 minutes before cooking.

2 Warm the redcurrant jelly in a bowl standing over a pan of gently simmering water and stir until smooth. Add the lime rind and sherry to the bowl and stir well until blended.

3 Lightly rinse the sardines and pat dry with absorbent kitchen paper.

4 Place on a chopping board and, with a sharp knife, make several diagonal cuts across the flesh of each fish. Season the sardines inside the cavities with salt and pepper.

5 Gently brush the warm marinade over the skin and inside the cavities of the sardines.

6 Place on the grill rack and cook under the preheated grill for 8–10 minutes, or until the fish are cooked.

7 Carefully turn the sardines over at least once during grilling. Baste occasionally with the remaining redcurrant and lime marinade. Garnish with the redcurrants. Serve immediately with the salad and lime wedges.

Ingredients   SERVES 4

2 tbsp redcurrant jelly
finely grated rind of 1 lime
2 tbsp medium dry sherry
450 g /1 lb fresh sardines,
    cleaned and heads removed
sea salt and freshly ground
    black pepper
lime wedges, to garnish

To serve:
fresh redcurrants
fresh green salad

Helpful hint
Most fish are sold cleaned but it is easy to do yourself. Using the back of a knife, scrape off the scales from the tail towards the head. Make a small slit along the belly using a sharp knife. Carefully scrape out the entrails and rinse thoroughly under cold running water. Pat dry with absorbent paper.

Gingered Cod Steaks

1 Preheat the grill and line the grill rack with a layer of foil. Coarsely grate the piece of ginger. Trim the spring onions and cut into thin strips.

2 Mix the spring onions, ginger, chopped parsley and sugar. Add 1 tablespoon of water.

3 Wipe the fish steaks. Season to taste with salt and pepper. Place onto 4 separate 20.5 x 20.5 cm/8 x 8 inch foil squares.

4 Carefully spoon the spring onion and ginger mixture over the fish.

5 Cut the butter into small cubes and place over the fish.

6 Loosely fold the foil over the steaks to enclose the fish and to make a parcel.

7 Place under the preheated grill and cook for 10–12 minutes or until cooked and the flesh has turned opaque.

8 Place the fish parcels on individual serving plates. Serve immediately with the freshly cooked vegetables.

Ingredients   SERVES 4

2.5 cm/1 inch piece fresh root
    ginger, peeled
4 spring onions
2 tsp freshly chopped parsley
1 tbsp soft brown sugar
4 x 175 g/6 oz thick cod steaks
salt and freshly ground black pepper
25 g/1 oz half-fat butter
freshly cooked vegetables, to serve

Tasty tip

Why not serve this dish with roasted new potatoes en papillote. Place the new potatoes into double thickness greaseproof paper with a few cloves of peeled garlic. Drizzle with a little olive oil and season well with salt and black pepper. Fold all the edges of the greaseproof paper together and roast in the oven at 180°C/350°F/Gas Mark 4 for 40–50 minutes before serving in the paper casing.

Smoked Mackerel & Potato Salad

1   Place the mustard powder and egg yolk in a small bowl with salt and pepper and whisk until blended. Add the oil, drop by drop, into the egg mixture, whisking continuously. When the mayonnaise is thick, add the lemon juice, drop by drop, until a smooth, glossy consistency is formed. Reserve.

2   Cook the potatoes in boiling salted water until tender, then drain. Cool slightly, then cut into halves or quarters, depending on size. Return to the saucepan and toss in the butter.

3   Remove the skin from the mackerel fillets and flake into pieces. Add to the potatoes in the saucepan, together with the celery.

4   Blend 4 tablespoons of the mayonnaise with the horseradish and crème fraîche. Season to taste with salt and pepper, then add to the potato and mackerel mixture and stir lightly.

5   Arrange the lettuce and tomatoes on 4 serving plates. Pile the smoked mackerel mixture on top of the lettuce, grind over a little pepper and serve with the remaining mayonnaise.

Ingredients   SERVES 4

$^1/_2$ tsp dry mustard powder
1 large egg yolk
salt and freshly ground black pepper
150 ml/$^1/_4$ pint sunflower oil
1–2 tbsp lemon juice
450 g/1 lb baby new potatoes
25 g/1 oz butter
350 g/12 oz smoked mackerel fillets
4 celery stalks, trimmed and
   finely chopped
3 tbsp creamed horseradish
150 ml/$^1/_4$ pint crème fraîche
1 little gem lettuce, rinsed and
   roughly torn
8 cherry tomatoes, halved

Helpful hint

When making mayonnaise, ensure that the ingredients are at room temperature, or it may curdle. For speed, it can be made in a food processor: briefly blend the mustard, yolk, seasoning and lemon juice then, with the motor running, slowly pour in the oil.

Battered Cod & Chunky Chips

1 Dissolve the yeast with a little of the beer in a jug and mix to a paste. Pour in the remaining beer, whisking all the time until smooth. Place the flour and salt in a bowl and gradually pour in the beer mixture, whisking continuously to make a thick, smooth batter. Cover the bowl and allow the batter to stand at room temperature for 1 hour.

2 Peel the potatoes and cut into thick slices. Cut each slice lengthways to make chunky chips. Place them in a non-stick frying pan and heat, shaking the pan until all the moisture has evaporated. Turn them onto absorbent kitchen paper to dry off.

3 Heat the oil to 180°C/350°F, then fry the chips a few at a time for 4–5 minutes until crisp and golden. Drain on absorbent kitchen paper and keep warm.

4 Pat the cod fillets dry, then coat in the flour. Dip the floured fillets into the reserved batter. Fry for 2–3 minutes until cooked and crisp, then drain. Garnish with lemon wedges and parsley and serve immediately with the chips, tomato ketchup and vinegar.

Ingredients   SERVES 4

15 g/¹/₂ oz fresh yeast
300 ml/¹/₂ pint beer
225 g/8 oz plain flour
1 tsp salt
700 g/1¹/₂ lb potatoes
450 ml/³/₄ pint groundnut oil
4 cod fillets, about 225 g/8 oz each, skinned and boned
2 tbsp seasoned plain flour

To garnish:
lemon wedges
sprigs of flat-leaf parsley

To serve:
tomato ketchup
vinegar

Helpful hint
Fresh yeast can be bought in health food shops, supermarkets with bakeries, and some bakers. Check that it is moist and creamy-coloured and has a strong yeasty smell. If it is dry, discoloured and crumbly, it is probably stale and will not work well.

Stir-fried Salmon with Peas

1 Wipe and skin the salmon fillet and remove any pin bones. Slice into 2.5 cm/1 inch strips, place on a dish and sprinkle with salt. Leave for 20 minutes, then pat dry with absorbent kitchen paper and reserve.

2 Remove any cartilage from the bacon, cut into small dice and reserve.

3 Heat a wok or large frying pan over a high heat, then add the oil and, when hot, add the bacon and stir-fry for 3 minutes or until crisp and golden. Push to one side and add the strips of salmon. Stir-fry gently for 2 minutes or until the flesh is opaque.

4 Pour the chicken or fish stock, soy sauce and Chinese rice wine or sherry into the wok, then stir in the sugar, peas and freshly shredded mint.

5 Blend the cornflour with 1 tablespoon of water to form a smooth paste and stir into the sauce. Bring to the boil, reduce the heat and simmer for 1 minute, or until slightly thickened and smooth. Garnish and serve immediately with noodles.

Ingredients   SERVES 4

450 g/1 lb salmon fillet
salt
6 slices streaky bacon
1 tbsp vegetable oil
50 ml/2 fl oz chicken or fish stock
2 tbsp dark soy sauce
2 tbsp Chinese rice wine or dry sherry
1 tsp sugar
75 g/3 oz frozen peas, thawed
1–2 tbsp freshly shredded mint
1 tsp cornflour
sprigs of fresh mint, to garnish
freshly cooked noodles, to serve

Helpful hint

Sprinkling salmon with salt draws out some of the juices and makes the flesh firmer, so that it remains whole when cooked. Prior to cooking, pat the strips with absorbent kitchen paper to remove as much of the salty liquid as possible. Dark soy sauce is used in this recipe as it is slightly less salty than the light version.

Fresh Tuna Salad

1 Wash the salad leaves and place in a large salad bowl with the cherry tomatoes and rocket and reserve.

2 Heat the wok, then add the oil and heat until almost smoking. Add the tuna, skin-side down, and cook for 4–6 minutes, turning once during cooking, or until cooked and the flesh flakes easily. Remove from the heat and leave to stand in the juices for 2 minutes before removing.

3 Meanwhile, make the dressing. Place the olive oil, lemon zest and juices and mustard in a small bowl or screw-top jar and whisk or shake well until blended. Season to taste with salt and pepper.

4 Transfer the tuna to a clean chopping board and flake, then add it to the salad and toss lightly.

5 Using a swivel blade vegetable peeler, peel the piece of Parmesan cheese into shavings. Divide the salad between 4 large serving plates, drizzle the dressing over the salad, then scatter with the Parmesan shavings.

Ingredients   SERVES 4

225 g/8 oz mixed salad leaves
225 g/8 oz baby cherry tomatoes, halved lengthways
125 g/4 oz rocket leaves, washed
2 tbsp groundnut oil
550 g/1$^1/_4$ lb boned tuna steaks, each cut into 4 small pieces
50 g/2 oz piece fresh Parmesan cheese

For the dressing:

8 tbsp olive oil
juice and grated zest of 2 small lemons
1 tbsp wholegrain mustard
salt and freshly ground black pepper

Helpful hint

Bags of mixed salad leaves are available from all major supermarkets. Although they seem expensive, there is very little waste and they do save time. Rinse the leaves before using.

Szechuan Chilli Prawns

1 Peel the prawns, leaving the tails attached if liked. Using a sharp knife, remove the black vein along the back of the prawns. Rinse and pat dry with absorbent kitchen paper.

2 Heat a wok or large frying pan, add the oil and, when hot, add the onion, pepper and chilli and stir-fry for 4–5 minutes, or until the vegetables are tender but retain a bite. Stir in the garlic and cook for 30 seconds. Using a slotted spoon, transfer to a plate and reserve.

3 Add the prawns to the wok and stir-fry for 1–2 minutes, or until they turn pink and opaque.

4 Blend all the chilli sauce ingredients together in a bowl or jug, then stir into the prawns. Add the reserved vegetables and bring to the boil, stirring constantly. Cook for 1–2 minutes, or until the sauce is thickened and the prawns and vegetables are well coated.

5 Stir in the spring onions, tip on to a warmed platter and garnish with chilli flowers or coriander sprigs. Serve immediately with freshly cooked rice or noodles.

Ingredients
SERVES 4

450 g/1 lb raw tiger prawns
2 tbsp groundnut oil
1 onion, peeled and sliced
1 red pepper, deseeded and
    cut into strips
1 small red chilli, deseeded
    and thinly sliced
2 garlic cloves, peeled and
    finely chopped
2–3 spring onions, trimmed
    and diagonally sliced
freshly cooked rice or noodles,
    to serve
sprigs of fresh coriander or chilli
    flowers, to garnish

For the chilli sauce:
1 tbsp cornflour
4 tbsp cold fish stock or water
2 tbsp soy sauce
2 tbsp sweet or hot chilli sauce,
    or to taste
2 tsp soft light brown sugar

Supreme Baked Potatoes

1 Preheat the oven to 200°C/400°F/Gas Mark 6. Scrub the potatoes and prick all over with a fork, or thread 2 potatoes onto 2 long metal skewers. Place the potatoes in the preheated oven for 1–1½ hours, or until soft to the touch.

2 Just before the potatoes are finished cooking, heat the oil in a frying pan and cook the carrot and celery for 2 minutes. Cover the pan tightly and continue to cook for another 5 minutes, or until the vegetables are tender.

3 When cooked, take the potatoes out of the oven and allow to cool a little, then cut in half. Scoop out the cooked potato and turn into a bowl, leaving a reasonably firm potato shell. Mash the cooked potato flesh, then mix in the butter and mash until the butter has melted.

4 Add the cooked vegetables to the bowl of mashed potato and mix well. Fold in the crab meat and the spring onions, then season to taste with salt and pepper.

5 Pile the mixture back into the potato shells and press in firmly. Sprinkle the grated cheese over the top and return the potato halves to the oven for 12–15 minutes until hot, golden and bubbling. Serve immediately with a tomato salad.

Ingredients   SERVES 4

4 large baking potatoes
40 g/1½ oz butter
1 tbsp sunflower oil
1 carrot, peeled and chopped
2 celery stalks, trimmed and
   finely chopped
200 g can white crab meat
2 spring onions, trimmed and
   finely chopped
salt and freshly ground black pepper
50 g/2 oz Cheddar cheese, grated
tomato salad, to serve

Tasty tip

Threading the potatoes onto metal skewers helps them to cook more evenly and quickly as heat is transferred via the metal to the centres of the potatoes during cooking. To give the skins a crunchier finish, rub them with a little oil and lightly sprinkle with salt before baking.

Warm Chicken & Potato Salad with Peas & Mint

1 Cook the potatoes in lightly salted boiling water for 15 minutes, or until just tender when pierced with the tip of a sharp knife; do not overcook. Rinse under cold running water to cool slightly, then drain and turn into a large bowl. Sprinkle with the cider vinegar and toss gently.

2 Run the peas under hot water to ensure that they are thawed, pat dry with absorbent kitchen paper and add to the potatoes.

3 Cut the avocado in half lengthways and remove the stone. Peel and cut the avocado into cubes and add to the potatoes and peas. Add the chicken and stir together lightly.

4 To make the dressing, place all the ingredients in a screw-top jar with a little salt and pepper and shake well to mix; add a little more oil if the flavour is too sharp. Pour over the salad and toss gently to coat. Sprinkle in half the mint and stir lightly.

5 Separate the lettuce leaves and spread onto a large shallow serving plate. Spoon the salad on top and sprinkle with the remaining mint. Garnish with mint sprigs and serve.

Ingredients   SERVES 4–6

450 g/1 lb new potatoes,
    peeled or scrubbed and
    cut into bite-size pieces
salt and freshly ground black pepper
2 tbsp cider vinegar
175 g/6 oz frozen garden peas, thawed
1 small ripe avocado
4 cooked chicken breasts, about
    450 g/1 lb in weight, skinned
    and diced
2 tbsp freshly chopped mint
2 heads little gem lettuce
fresh mint sprigs, to garnish

For the dressing:

2 tbsp raspberry or sherry vinegar
2 tsp Dijon mustard
1 tsp clear honey
50 ml/2 fl oz sunflower oil
50 ml/2 fl oz extra virgin olive oil

Turkey & Vegetable Stir-fry

1. Slice or chop the vegetables into small pieces, depending on which you use. Halve the baby sweetcorn lengthways, deseed and thinly slice the red pepper, tear or shred the pak choi, slice the mushrooms, break the broccoli into small florets and cut the carrots into matchsticks. Deseed and finely chop the chilli.

2. Heat a wok or large frying pan, add the oil and when hot, add the turkey strips and stir-fry for 1 minute or until they turn white. Add the garlic, ginger, spring onions and chilli and cook for a few seconds.

3. Add the prepared carrot, pepper, broccoli and mushrooms and stir-fry for 1 minute. Add the baby sweetcorn and pak choi and stir-fry for 1 minute.

4. Blend the soy sauce, Chinese rice wine or sherry and stock or water and pour over the vegetables. Blend the cornflour with 1 teaspoon of water and stir into the vegetables, mixing well. Bring to the boil, reduce the heat, then simmer for 1 minute. Stir in the sesame oil. Tip into a warmed serving dish, sprinkle with cashew nuts, shredded spring onions and bean sprouts. Serve immediately with noodles or rice.

Ingredients   SERVES 4

350 g/12 oz mixed vegetables, such as baby sweetcorn, 1 small red pepper, pak choi, mushrooms, broccoli florets and baby carrots
1 red chilli
2 tbsp groundnut oil
350 g/12 oz skinless, boneless turkey breast, sliced into fine strips across the grain
2 garlic cloves, peeled and finely chopped
2.5 cm/1 inch piece fresh root ginger, peeled and finely grated
3 spring onions, trimmed and finely sliced
2 tbsp light soy sauce
1 tbsp Chinese rice wine or dry sherry
2 tbsp chicken stock or water
1 tsp cornflour
1 tsp sesame oil
freshly cooked noodles or rice, to serve

To garnish:
50 g/2 oz toasted cashew nuts
2 spring onions, finely shredded
25 g/1 oz bean sprouts

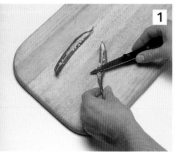

Turkey Hash with Potato & Beetroot

1 In a large, heavy-based frying pan, heat the oil and half the butter over a medium heat until sizzling. Add the bacon and cook for 4 minutes, or until crisp and golden, stirring occasionally. Using a slotted spoon, transfer to a large bowl. Add the onion to the pan and cook for 3–4 minutes, or until soft and golden, stirring frequently.

2 Meanwhile, add the turkey, potatoes, parsley and flour to the cooked bacon in the bowl. Stir and toss gently, then fold in the diced beetroot.

3 Add half the remaining butter to the frying pan and then the turkey vegetable mixture. Stir, then spread the mixture to evenly cover the bottom of the frying pan. Cook for 15 minutes, or until the underside is crisp and brown, pressing the hash firmly into a cake with a spatula. Remove from the heat.

4 Invert a large plate over the frying pan and, holding the plate and frying pan together with an oven glove, turn the hash out onto the plate. Heat the remaining butter in the pan, slide the hash back into the pan and cook for 4 minutes, or until crisp and brown on the other side. Invert onto the plate again and serve immediately with a green salad.

Ingredients   SERVES 4–6

2 tbsp vegetable oil
50 g/2 oz butter
4 slices streaky bacon, diced or sliced
1 medium onion, peeled and
    finely chopped
450 g/1 lb cooked turkey, diced
450 g/1 lb finely chopped
    cooked potatoes
2–3 tbsp freshly chopped parsley
2 tbsp plain flour
250 g/9 oz cooked medium
    beetroot, diced
green salad, to serve

Tasty tip

A hash is usually made just with potatoes, but here they are combined with ruby red beetroot, which adds vibrant colour and a sweet earthy flavour to the dish. Make sure that you buy plainly cooked beetroot, rather than the type preserved in vinegar.

Beef Fajitas with Avocado Sauce

1 Heat the wok, add the oil, then stir-fry the beef for 3–4 minutes. Add the garlic and spices and continue to cook for a further 2 minutes. Stir the tomatoes into the wok, bring to the boil, cover and simmer gently for 5 minutes.

2 Meanwhile, blend the kidney beans in a food processor until slightly broken up, then add to the wok. Continue to cook for a further 5 minutes, adding 2–3 tablespoons of water. The mixture should be thick and fairly dry. Stir in the chopped coriander.

3 Mix the chopped avocado, shallot, tomato, chilli and lemon juice together. Spoon into a serving dish and reserve.

4 When ready to serve, warm the tortillas and spread with a little soured cream. Place a spoonful of the beef mixture on top, followed by a spoonful of the avocado sauce, then roll up. Repeat until all the mixture is used up. Serve immediately with a green salad.

Ingredients
SERVES 3–6

2 tbsp sunflower oil

450 g/1 lb beef fillet or rump steak, trimmed and cut into thin strips

2 garlic cloves, peeled and crushed

1 tsp ground cumin

$^1/_4$ tsp cayenne pepper

1 tbsp paprika

230 g can chopped tomatoes

215 g can red kidney beans, drained

1 tbsp freshly chopped coriander

1 avocado, peeled, pitted and chopped

1 shallot, peeled and chopped

1 large tomato, skinned, deseeded and chopped

1 red chilli, diced

1 tbsp lemon juice

6 large flour tortilla pancakes

3–4 tbsp soured cream

green salad, to serve

Helpful hint

The avocado sauce should not be made too far in advance, as it has a tendency to discolour. If it is made it ahead, it should be covered with clingfilm.

Pasta with Beef, Capers & Olives

1   Heat the olive oil in a large frying pan over a high heat. Add the steak and cook, stirring, for 3–4 minutes, or until browned. Remove from the pan using a slotted spoon and reserve.

2   Lower the heat, add the spring onions and garlic to the pan and cook for 1 minute. Add the courgettes and pepper and cook for 3–4 minutes.

3   Add the oregano, capers and olives to the pan with the chopped tomatoes. Season to taste with salt and pepper, then simmer for 7 minutes, stirring occasionally. Return the beef to the pan and simmer for 3–5 minutes, or until the sauce has thickened slightly.

4   Meanwhile, bring a large pan of lightly salted water to a rolling boil. Add the pasta and cook according to the packet instructions, or until 'al dente'.

5   Drain the pasta thoroughly. Return to the pan and add the beef sauce. Toss gently until the pasta is lightly coated. Tip into a warmed serving dish or onto individual plates. Sprinkle with chopped parsley and serve immediately.

Ingredients   SERVES 4

2 tbsp olive oil
300 g/11 oz rump steak,
    trimmed and cut into strips
4 spring onions, trimmed and sliced
2 garlic cloves, peeled and chopped
2 courgettes, trimmed and cut
    into strips
1 red pepper, deseeded and cut
    into strips
2 tsp freshly chopped oregano
2 tbsp capers, drained and rinsed
4 tbsp pitted black olives, sliced
400 g can chopped tomatoes
salt and freshly ground black pepper
450 g/1 lb fettuccine
1 tbsp freshly chopped parsley,
    to garnish

Tasty tip

Make sure that the oil in the pan is hot so that the strips of beef sizzle when added. Pat the beef dry with kitchen paper and cook it in two batches. Reserve the first batch on a plate, then return to the pan with any juices.

Chilli Beef

1 Using a sharp knife, trim the beef, discarding any fat or gristle, then cut into thin strips and place in a shallow dish. Combine all the marinade ingredients in a bowl and pour over the beef. Turn the beef in the marinade until coated evenly, cover with clingfilm and leave to marinate in the refrigerator for at least 30 minutes.

2 Heat a wok or large frying pan, add the groundnut oil and heat until almost smoking, then add the carrots and stir-fry for 3–4 minutes, or until softened. Add the mangetout and stir-fry for a further 1 minute. Using a slotted spoon, transfer the vegetables to a plate and keep warm.

3 Lift the beef strips from the marinade, shaking to remove excess marinade. Reserve the marinade. Add the beef to the wok and stir-fry for 3 minutes or until browned all over.

4 Return the stir-fried vegetables to the wok together with the bean sprouts, chilli and sesame seeds and cook for 1 minute. Stir in the reserved marinade and stir-fry for 1–2 minutes or until heated through. Tip into a warmed serving dish or spoon onto individual plates and serve immediately with freshly cooked rice.

Ingredients   SERVES 4

550 g/1¼ lb beef rump steak
2 tbsp groundnut oil
2 carrots, peeled and cut
    into matchsticks
125 g/4 oz mangetout, shredded
125 g/4 oz bean sprouts
1 green chilli, deseeded
    and chopped
2 tbsp sesame seeds
freshly cooked rice, to serve

For the marinade:

1 garlic clove, peeled and chopped
3 tbsp soy sauce
1 tbsp sweet chilli sauce
4 tbsp groundnut oil

Food fact

Chilli sauce is a mixture of crushed fresh chillies, plums, vinegar and salt. It is available in several varieties: extra hot, hot or sweet, as used here, which is the mildest version.

Spaghetti Bolognese

1. Peel and chop the carrot, trim and chop the celery, then peel and chop the onion and garlic. Heat a large non-stick frying pan and sauté the beef and bacon for 5–10 minutes, stirring occasionally, until browned. Add the prepared vegetables to the frying pan and cook for about 3 minutes, or until softened, stirring occasionally.

2. Add the flour and cook for 1 minute. Stir in the red wine, tomatoes, tomato purée, mixed herbs, seasoning to taste and sugar. Bring to the boil, then cover and simmer for 45 minutes, stirring occasionally.

3. Meanwhile, bring a large saucepan of lightly salted water to the boil and cook the spaghetti for 10–12 minutes, or until 'al dente'. Drain well and divide between 4 serving plates. Spoon over the sauce, garnish with a few sprigs of oregano and serve immediately with plenty of Parmesan shavings.

Ingredients   SERVES 4

1 carrot

2 celery stalks

1 onion

2 garlic cloves

450 g/1 lb lean minced beef steak

225 g/8 oz smoked streaky
   bacon, chopped

1 tbsp plain flour

150 ml/$^1/_4$ pint red wine

379 g can chopped tomatoes

2 tbsp tomato purée

2 tsp dried mixed herbs

salt and freshly ground black pepper

pinch of sugar

350 g/12 oz spaghetti

sprigs of fresh oregano, to garnish

shavings of Parmesan cheese, to serve

Tasty tip

Layer up the sauce with sheets of lasagne and top with a ready-made bechamel sauce and Parmesan cheese. Bake for 30–40 minutes in a preheated oven at 190°C/375°F/Gas Mark 5, or until bubbling and the top is golden.

Shepherd's Pie

1 Preheat the oven to 200°C/400°F/Gas Mark 6, about 15 minutes before cooking. Heat the oil in a large saucepan and add the onion, carrot and celery. Cook over a medium heat for 8–10 minutes until softened and starting to brown.

2 Add the thyme and cook briefly, then add the cooked lamb, wine, stock and tomato purée. Season to taste with salt and pepper and simmer gently for 25–30 minutes until reduced and thickened. Remove from the heat to cool slightly and season again.

3 Meanwhile, boil the potatoes in plenty of salted water for 12–15 minutes until tender. Drain and return to the saucepan over a low heat to dry out. Remove from the heat and add the butter, milk and parsley. Mash until creamy, adding a little more milk, if necessary. Adjust the seasoning.

4 Transfer the lamb mixture to a shallow ovenproof dish. Spoon the mash over the filling and spread evenly to cover completely. Fork the surface, place on a baking sheet, then cook in the preheated oven for 25–30 minutes until the potato topping is browned and the filling is piping hot. Garnish and serve.

Ingredients   SERVES 4

2 tbsp vegetable or olive oil
1 onion, peeled and finely chopped
1 carrot, peeled and finely chopped
1 celery stalk, trimmed and
    finely chopped
1 tbsp sprigs of fresh thyme
450 g/1 lb leftover roast lamb,
    finely chopped
150 ml/¼ pint red wine
150 ml/¼ pint lamb or vegetable
    stock or leftover gravy
2 tbsp tomato purée
salt and freshly ground black pepper
700 g/1½ lb potatoes, peeled and
    cut into chunks
25 g/1 oz butter
6 tbsp milk
1 tbsp freshly chopped parsley
fresh herbs, to garnish

Tasty tip

Make it with fresh minced lamb. Simply dry-fry 450 g/1 lb lean mince over a high heat until well-browned, then follow the recipe as before.

Lamb Arrabbiata

1 Heat 2 tablespoons of the olive oil in a large frying pan and cook the lamb for 5–7 minutes, or until sealed. Remove from the pan using a slotted spoon and reserve.

2 Heat the remaining oil in the pan, add the onion, garlic and chilli and cook until softened. Add the tomatoes, bring to the boil, then simmer for 10 minutes.

3 Return the browned lamb to the pan with the olives and pour in the wine. Bring the sauce back to the boil, reduce the heat then simmer, uncovered, for 15 minutes, until the lamb is tender. Season to taste with salt and pepper.

4 Meanwhile, bring a large pan of lightly salted water to a rolling boil. Add the pasta and cook according to the packet instructions, or until 'al dente'.

5 Drain the pasta, toss in the butter, then add to the sauce and mix lightly. Stir in 4 tablespoons of the chopped parsley, then tip into a warmed serving dish. Sprinkle with the remaining parsley and serve immediately.

Ingredients SERVES 4

4 tbsp olive oil
450 g/1 lb lamb fillets, cubed
1 large onion, peeled and sliced
4 garlic cloves, peeled and
    finely chopped
1 red chilli, deseeded and
    finely chopped
400 g can chopped tomatoes
175 g/6 oz pitted black olives, halved
150 ml/$^1/_4$ pint white wine
salt and freshly ground black pepper
275 g/10 oz farfalle pasta
1 tsp butter
4 tbsp freshly chopped parsley,
    plus 1 tbsp to garnish

Food fact

When cooking pasta, remember to use a very large saucepan so that the pasta has plenty of room to move around freely. Once the water has come to the boil, add the pasta, stir, cover with a lid and return to the boil. The lid can then be removed so that the water does not boil over.

Chilli Lamb

1 Trim the lamb fillet, discarding any fat or sinew, then place it on a clean chopping board and cut into thin strips. Heat a wok and pour in 2 tablespoons of the groundnut oil and, when hot, stir-fry the lamb for 3–4 minutes, or until it is browned. Remove the lamb strips with their juices and reserve.

2 Add the remaining oil to the wok, then stir-fry the onion and garlic for 2 minutes, or until softened. Remove with a slotted spoon and add to the lamb.

3 Blend the cornflour with 125 ml/4 fl oz of cold water, then stir in the chilli sauce, vinegar, sugar and Chinese five-spice powder. Pour this into the wok, turn up the heat and bring the mixture to the boil. Cook for 30 seconds or until the sauce thickens.

4 Return the lamb to the wok with the onion and garlic, stir thoroughly and heat through until piping hot. Garnish with sprigs of fresh coriander and serve immediately with freshly cooked noodles, topped with a spoonful of Greek yogurt.

Ingredients SERVES 4

550 g/1¼ lb lamb fillet
3 tbsp groundnut oil
1 large onion, peeled and
   finely sliced
2 garlic cloves, peeled and crushed
4 tsp cornflour
4 tbsp hot chilli sauce
2 tbsp white wine vinegar
4 tsp dark soft brown sugar
1 tsp Chinese five-spice powder
sprigs of fresh coriander, to garnish

To serve:
freshly cooked noodles
4 tbsp Greek-style yogurt

Helpful hint
It is important to use bottled hot chilli sauce rather than Tabasco in this recipe. Chilli sauce is less fiery, though still quite hot, so taste a tiny bit first, then adjust the quantity according to taste.

Hot Salami & Vegetable Gratin

1 Preheat oven to 200°C/400°F/Gas Mark 6. Peel and slice the carrots, trim the beans and asparagus and reserve. Cook the carrots in a saucepan of lightly salted boiling water for 5 minutes. Add the remaining vegetables, except the spinach, and cook for about a further 5 minutes, or until tender. Drain and place in an ovenproof dish.

2 Discard any skin from the outside of the salami, if necessary, then chop roughly. Heat the oil in a frying pan and fry the salami for 4–5 minutes, stirring occasionally, until golden. Using a slotted spoon, transfer the salami to the ovenproof dish and scatter over the mint.

3 Add the butter to the frying pan and cook the spinach for 1–2 minutes, or until just wilted. Stir in the double cream and season well with salt and pepper. Spoon the mixture over the vegetables.

4 Whizz the ciabatta loaf in a food processor to make breadcrumbs. Stir in the Parmesan cheese and sprinkle over the vegetables. Bake in the preheated oven for 20 minutes, until golden and heated through. Serve with a green salad.

Ingredients SERVES 4

350 g/12 oz carrots
175 g/6 oz fine green beans
250 g/9 oz asparagus tips
175 g/6 oz frozen peas
225 g/8 oz Italian salami
1 tbsp olive oil
1 tbsp freshly chopped mint
25 g/1 oz butter
150 g/5 oz baby spinach leaves
150 ml/$^1/_4$ pint double cream
salt and freshly ground black pepper
1 small or $^1/_2$ an olive ciabatta loaf
75 g/3 oz Parmesan cheese, grated
green salad, to serve

Tasty tip

Prepare this dish ahead up to the end of step 3 and refrigerate until ready to cook, then top with breadcrumbs and bake, adding about 5 minutes to the final cooking time.

Leek & Ham Risotto

1 Heat the oil and half the butter together in a large saucepan. Add the onion and leeks and cook over a medium heat for 6–8 minutes, stirring occasionally, until soft and beginning to colour. Stir in the thyme and cook briefly.

2 Add the rice and stir well. Continue stirring over a medium heat for about 1 minute until the rice is glossy. Add a ladleful or two of the stock and stir well until the stock is absorbed. Continue adding stock, a ladleful at a time, and stirring well between additions, until about two thirds of the stock has been added.

3 Meanwhile, either chop or finely shred the ham, then add to the saucepan of rice together with the peas. Continue adding ladlefuls of stock, as described in step 2, until the rice is tender and the ham is heated through thoroughly.

4 Add the remaining butter, sprinkle over the Parmesan cheese and season to taste with salt and pepper. When the butter has melted and the cheese has softened, stir well to incorporate. Taste and adjust the seasoning, then serve immediately.

Ingredients   SERVES 4

1 tbsp olive oil
25 g/1 oz butter
1 medium onion, peeled and
    finely chopped
4 leeks, trimmed and thinly sliced
$1^{1}/_{2}$ tbsp freshly chopped thyme
350 g/12 oz Arborio rice
1.4 litres/$2^{1}/_{4}$ pints vegetable or
    chicken stock, heated
225 g/8 oz cooked ham
175 g/6 oz peas, thawed if frozen
50 g/2 oz Parmesan cheese, grated
salt and freshly ground black pepper

Helpful hint

Risotto should take about 15 minutes to cook, so taste it after this time – the rice should be creamy with just a slight bite to it. If it is not quite ready, continue adding the stock, a little at a time, and cook for a few more minutes. Stop as soon as it tastes ready as you do not have to add all of the liquid.

Pork Sausages with Onion Gravy & Best-ever Mash

1 Melt the butter with the oil and add the onions. Cover and cook gently for about 20 minutes until the onions have collapsed. Add the sugar and stir well. Uncover and continue to cook, stirring often, until the onions are very soft and golden. Add the thyme, stir well, then add the flour, stirring. Gradually add the Madeira and the stock. Bring to the boil and simmer gently for 10 minutes.

2 Meanwhile, put the sausages in a large frying pan and cook over a medium heat for about 15–20 minutes, turning often, until golden brown and slightly sticky all over.

3 For the mash, boil the potatoes in plenty of lightly salted water for 15–18 minutes until tender. Drain well and return to the saucepan. Put the saucepan over a low heat to allow the potatoes to dry thoroughly. Remove from the heat and add the butter, crème fraîche and salt and pepper. Mash thoroughly. Serve the potato mash topped with the sausages and onion gravy.

Ingredients SERVES 4

50 g/2 oz butter

1 tbsp olive oil

2 large onions, peeled and thinly sliced

pinch of sugar

1 tbsp freshly chopped thyme

1 tbsp plain flour

100 ml/3^{1}/$_{2}$ fl oz Madeira

200 ml/7 fl oz vegetable stock

8–12 good quality butchers' pork
 sausages, depending on size

For the mash:

900 g/2 lb floury potatoes, peeled

75 g/3 oz butter

4 tbsp crème fraîche or soured cream

salt and freshly ground black pepper

Helpful hint

There is a huge range of regional pork sausages to choose from. Try meaty Cambridge sausages packed with herbs and spices, or Cumberland sausages made from coarsely chopped pork and black pepper.

Pasta & Pork Ragù

1 Heat the sunflower oil in a large frying pan. Add the sliced leek and cook, stirring frequently, for 5 minutes, or until softened. Add the pork and cook, stirring, for 4 minutes, or until sealed.

2 Add the crushed garlic, paprika and cayenne pepper to the pan and stir until all the pork is lightly coated in the garlic and pepper mixture.

3 Pour in the wine and 450 ml/³/₄ pint of the vegetable stock. Add the borlotti beans and carrots and season to taste with salt and pepper. Bring the sauce to the boil, then lower the heat and simmer for 5 minutes.

4 Meanwhile, place the egg tagliatelle in a large saucepan of lightly salted, boiling water, cover and simmer for 5 minutes, or until the pasta is cooked 'al dente'.

5 Drain the pasta, then add to the pork ragù and toss well. Adjust the seasoning, then tip into a warmed serving dish. Sprinkle with chopped parsley and serve with a little crème fraîche.

Ingredients   SERVES 4

1 tbsp sunflower oil
1 leek, trimmed and thinly sliced
225 g/8 oz pork fillet, diced
1 garlic clove, peeled and crushed
2 tsp paprika
¹/₄ tsp cayenne pepper
150 ml/¹/₄ pint white wine
600 ml/1 pint vegetable stock
400 g can borlotti beans,
    drained and rinsed
2 carrots, peeled and diced
salt and freshly ground black pepper
225 g/8 oz fresh egg tagliatelle
1 tbsp freshly chopped parsley,
    to garnish
crème fraîche, to serve

Helpful hint

Pork fillet, also known as tenderloin, is a very lean and tender cut of pork. It needs little cooking time, so is perfect for this quick and simple dish. Rump or sirloin steak or boneless skinned chicken breast, cut into thin strips, could be used instead, if preferred.

Pork Goulash & Rice

1 Preheat the oven to 140°C/275°F/Gas Mark 1. Cut the pork into large cubes, about 4 cm/1½ inches square. Heat the oil in a large flameproof casserole and brown the pork in batches over a high heat, transferring the cubes to a plate as they brown.

2 Over a medium heat, add the onions and pepper and cook for about 5 minutes, stirring regularly, until they begin to brown. Add the garlic and return the meat to the casserole along with any juices on the plate. Sprinkle in the flour and paprika and stir well to soak up the oil and juices.

3 Add the tomatoes and season to taste with salt and pepper. Bring slowly to the boil, cover with a tight-fitting lid and cook in the preheated oven for 1½ hours.

4 Meanwhile, rinse the rice in several changes of water until the water remains relatively clear. Drain well and put into a saucepan with the chicken stock or water and a little salt. Cover tightly and bring to the boil. Turn the heat down as low as possible and cook for 10 minutes without removing the lid. After 10 minutes, remove from the heat and leave for a further 10 minutes, without removing the lid. Fluff with a fork.

5 When the meat is tender, stir in the soured cream lightly to create a marbled effect, or serve separately. Garnish with parsley and serve immediately with the rice.

Ingredients   SERVES 4

700 g/1½ lb boneless pork rib chops
1 tbsp olive oil
2 onions, peeled and
   roughly chopped
1 red pepper, deseeded and
   thinly sliced
1 garlic clove, peeled and crushed
1 tbsp plain flour
1 rounded tbsp paprika
400 g can chopped tomatoes
salt and freshly ground black pepper
250 g/9 oz long-grain white rice
450 ml/¾ pint chicken stock
sprigs of fresh flat-leaf parsley,
   to garnish
150 ml/¼ pint soured cream,
   to serve

Food fact

Paprika is the ground red powder from the dried pepper Capsicum annum and is a vital ingredient of goulash, giving it a distinctive colour and taste.

Sweetcorn Fritters

1 Heat 1 tablespoon of the groundnut oil in a frying pan, add the onion and cook gently for 7–8 minutes or until beginning to soften. Add the chilli, garlic and ground coriander and cook for 1 minute, stirring continuously. Remove from the heat.

2 Drain the sweetcorn and tip into a mixing bowl. Lightly mash with a potato masher to break down the corn a little. Add the cooked onion mixture to the bowl with the spring onions and beaten egg. Season to taste with salt and pepper, then stir to mix together. Sift the flour and baking powder over the mixture and stir in.

3 Heat 2 tablespoons of the groundnut oil in a large frying pan. Drop 4 or 5 heaped teaspoonfuls of the sweetcorn mixture into the pan and, using a fish slice or spatula, flatten each to make a 1 cm/$^1/_2$ inch thick fritter.

4 Fry the fritters for 3 minutes, or until golden brown on the underside, turn over and fry for a further 3 minutes, or until cooked through and crisp.

5 Remove the fritters from the pan and drain on absorbent kitchen paper. Keep warm while cooking the remaining fritters, adding a little more oil if needed. Garnish with spring onion curls and serve immediately with a Thai-style chutney.

Ingredients   SERVES 4

4 tbsp groundnut oil

1 small onion, peeled and finely chopped

1 red chilli, deseeded and finely chopped

1 garlic clove, peeled and crushed

1 tsp ground coriander

325 g can sweetcorn

6 spring onions, trimmed and finely sliced

1 medium egg, lightly beaten

salt and freshly ground black pepper

3 tbsp plain flour

1 tsp baking powder

spring onion curls, to garnish

Thai-style chutney, to serve

Helpful hint

To make a spring onion curl, trim off the root and some green top to leave 10 cm/4 inches. Make a 3 cm/1$^1/_4$ inch cut down from the top, then make another cut at a right angle to the first cut. Continue making fine cuts. Soak the spring onions in iced water for 20 minutes.

Tagliatelle with Broccoli & Sesame

1 Bring a large saucepan of salted water to the boil and add the broccoli and corn. Return the water to the boil then remove the vegetables at once using a slotted spoon, reserving the water. Plunge them into cold water and drain well. Dry on kitchen paper and reserve.

2 Return the water to the boil. Add the tagliatelle and cook until 'al dente' or according to the packet instructions. Drain well. Run under cold water until cold, then drain well again.

3 Place the tahini, soy sauce, sugar and vinegar into a bowl. Mix well, then reserve. Heat the oil in a wok or large frying pan over a high heat and add the garlic, ginger and chilli flakes and stir-fry for about 30 seconds. Add the broccoli and baby corn and continue to stir-fry for about 3 minutes.

4 Add the tagliatelle to the wok along with the tahini mixture and stir together for a further 1–2 minutes until heated through. Season to taste with salt and pepper. Sprinkle with sesame seeds, garnish with the radish slices and serve immediately.

Ingredients   SERVES 2

225 g/8 oz broccoli, cut into florets
125 g/4 oz baby corn
175 g/6 oz dried tagliatelle
$1^1/_2$ tbsp tahini paste
1 tbsp dark soy sauce
1 tbsp dark muscovado sugar
1 tbsp red wine vinegar
1 tbsp sunflower oil
1 garlic clove, peeled and
    finely chopped
2.5 cm/1 inch piece fresh root
    ginger, peeled and shredded
$^1/_2$ tsp dried chilli flakes
salt and freshly ground black pepper
1 tbsp toasted sesame seeds
slices of radish, to garnish

Food fact
Tahini is made from ground sesame seeds and is generally available in large supermarkets and Middle Eastern shops. It is most often used in hummus.

Vegetable Biryani

1 Preheat the oven to 200°C/400°F/Gas Mark 6. Put 1 tablespoon of the vegetable oil in a large bowl with the onions and toss to coat. Lightly brush or spray a non-stick baking sheet with a little more oil. Spread half the onions onto the baking sheet and cook at the top of the preheated oven for 25–30 minutes, stirring regularly, until golden and crisp. Remove from the oven and reserve for the garnish.

2 Meanwhile, heat a large flameproof casserole over a medium heat and add the remaining oil and onions. Cook for 5–7 minutes until softened and starting to brown. Add a little water if they start to stick. Add the garlic and ginger and cook for another minute, then add the carrot, parsnip and sweet potato. Cook the vegetables for a further 5 minutes. Add the curry paste and stir for 1 minute until everything is coated, then stir in the rice and tomatoes. After 2 minutes add the stock and stir well. Bring to the boil, cover and simmer over a very gentle heat for about 10 minutes.

3 Add the cauliflower and peas and cook for 8–10 minutes, or until the rice is tender. Season to taste with salt and pepper. Serve garnished with the crispy onions, cashew nuts, raisins and coriander.

Ingredients   SERVES 4

2 tbsp vegetable oil, plus a little extra
  for brushing
2 large onions, peeled and thinly
  sliced lengthways
2 garlic cloves, peeled and finely
  chopped
2.5 cm/1 inch piece fresh root ginger,
  peeled and finely grated
1 small carrot, peeled and cut into sticks
1 small parsnip, peeled and diced
1 small sweet potato, peeled and diced
1 tbsp medium curry paste
225 g/8 oz basmati rice
4 ripe tomatoes, peeled, deseeded
  and diced
600 ml/1 pint vegetable stock
175 g/6 oz cauliflower florets
50 g/2 oz peas, thawed if frozen
salt and freshly ground black pepper

To garnish:

roasted cashew nuts
raisins
fresh coriander leaves

Baked Aubergines with Tomato & Mozzarella

1 Preheat the oven to 200°C/400°F/Gas Mark 6, 15 minutes before cooking. Place the aubergine slices in a colander and sprinkle with salt. Leave for 1 hour or until the juices run clear. Rinse and dry on absorbent kitchen paper.

2 Heat 3–5 tablespoons of the olive oil in a large frying pan and cook the prepared aubergines in batches for 2 minutes on each side, or until softened. Remove and drain on absorbent kitchen paper.

3 Heat 1 tablespoon of olive oil in a saucepan, add the turkey mince and cook for 5 minutes, or until browned and sealed. Add the onion to the pan and cook for 5 minutes, or until softened. Add the chopped garlic, tomatoes and mixed herbs. Pour in the wine and season to taste with salt and pepper. Bring to the boil, lower the heat then simmer for 15 minutes, or until thickened.

4 Meanwhile, bring a large pan of lightly salted water to a rolling boil. Add the macaroni and cook according to the packet instructions, or until 'al dente'. Drain thoroughly.

5 Spoon half the tomato mixture into a lightly oiled ovenproof dish. Top with half the aubergines, pasta and chopped basil, then season lightly. Repeat the layers, finishing with a layer of aubergine. Sprinkle with the mozzarella and Parmesan cheeses, then bake in the preheated oven for 30 minutes, or until golden and bubbling. Serve immediately.

Ingredients   SERVES 4

3 medium aubergines, trimmed
    and sliced
salt and freshly ground black pepper
4–6 tbsp olive oil
450 g/1 lb fresh turkey mince
1 onion, peeled and chopped
2 garlic cloves, peeled and chopped
2 x 400 g cans cherry tomatoes
1 tbsp fresh mixed herbs
200 ml/7 fl oz red wine
350 g/12 oz macaroni
5 tbsp freshly chopped basil
125 g/4 oz mozzarella cheese,
    drained and chopped
50 g/2 oz freshly grated
    Parmesan cheese

Helpful hint

Aubergines are salted to remove bitterness, although they are now less bitter. Salting also removes moisture so they absorb less oil when fried.

Four-cheese Tagliatelle

1 Place the whipping cream with the garlic cloves in a medium pan and heat gently until small bubbles begin to form around the edge of the pan. Using a slotted spoon, remove and discard the garlic cloves.

2 Add all the cheeses to the pan and stir until melted. Season with a little salt and a lot of black pepper. Keep the sauce warm over a low heat, but do not allow to boil.

3 Meanwhile, bring a large pan of lightly salted water to the boil. Add the tagliatelle, return to the boil and cook for 2–3 minutes, or until 'al dente'.

4 Drain the pasta thoroughly and return to the pan. Pour the sauce over the pasta, add the chives then toss lightly until well coated. Tip into a warmed serving dish or spoon onto individual plates. Garnish with a few basil leaves and serve immediately with extra Parmesan cheese.

Ingredients   SERVES 4

300 ml/$^1/_2$ pint whipping cream
4 garlic cloves, peeled and
    lightly bruised
75 g/3 oz fontina cheese, diced
75 g/3 oz Gruyère cheese, grated
75 g/3 oz mozzarella cheese,
    preferably, diced
50 g/2 oz Parmesan cheese, grated,
    plus extra to serve
salt and freshly ground black pepper
275 g/10 oz fresh green tagliatelle
1–2 tbsp freshly snipped chives
fresh basil leaves, to garnish

Food fact

Tagliatelle comes from Bologna, where it is usually served with a meat sauce. Green tagliatelle is generally flavoured with spinach, but it is also available flavoured with fresh herbs, which would go particularly well with the rich cheese sauce in this recipe.

Prawn Skewers with Tomato Salsa

1   To make the marinade, place all the ingredients in a non-metallic bowl and whisk together. Set aside.

2   To prepare the prawns, break off the heads and peel off the shells, leaving the tails intact. Using a small knife, make a slit along the back and remove the thin black vein. Add the prawns to the marinade and stir until well coated. Cover and chill for 15 minutes.

3   Make the salsa. Put all the ingredients, except the basil, in a non-metallic bowl and toss together. Season to taste with salt and pepper.

4   Thread 4 prawns onto a metal skewer, bending each in half. Repeat with 7 more skewers. Brush with marinade.

5   Brush a grill rack with oil. Place the skewers on the rack, then position under a preheated hot grill, about 7.5 cm/3 inches from the heat and cook for 1 minute. Turn the skewers over, brush again and continue to cook for 1–1$^1/_2$ minutes until the prawns turn pink and opaque.

6   Tear the basil leaves and toss with the salsa. Arrange each skewer on a plate with some salsa and garnish with parsley. Serve with skordalia or aïoli dip.

Ingredients   SERVES 4

32 large tiger prawns
olive oil, for brushing
skordalia or aïoli, to serve

For the marinade:

120 ml/4 fl oz extra virgin olive oil
2 tbsp lemon juice
1 tsp red chilli, finely chopped
1 tsp balsamic vinegar
black pepper

For the tomato salsa:

2 large sun-ripened tomatoes,
    skinned, cored, deseeded and
    chopped
4 spring onions, white parts only,
    very finely chopped
1 red pepper, skinned, deseeded
    and chopped
1 orange or yellow pepper, skinned,
    deseeded and chopped
1 tbsp extra virgin olive oil
2 tsp balsamic vinegar
4 sprigs fresh basil

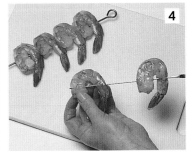

Sauvignon Chicken & Mushroom Filo Pie

1 Preheat the oven to 190°C/375°F/Gas Mark 5. Put the onion and leek in a heavy-based saucepan with 125 ml/4 fl oz of the stock. Bring to the boil, cover and simmer for 5 minutes, then uncover and cook until all the stock has evaporated and the vegetables are tender.

2 Cut the chicken into bite-size cubes. Add to the pan with the remaining stock, wine and bay leaf. Cover and gently simmer for 5 minutes. Add the mushrooms and simmer for a further 5 minutes.

3 Blend the flour with 3 tablespoons of cold water. Stir into the pan and cook, stirring all the time until the sauce has thickened. Stir the tarragon into the sauce and season with salt and pepper.

4 Spoon the mixture into a 1.2 litre/2 pint pie dish, discarding the bay leaf.

5 Lightly brush a sheet of filo pastry with a little of the oil. Crumple the pastry slightly. Arrange on top of the filling. Repeat with the remaining filo sheets and oil, then sprinkle the top of the pie with the sesame seeds.

6 Bake the pie on the middle shelf of the preheated oven for 20 minutes until the filo pastry topping is golden and crisp. Garnish with a sprig of parsley. Serve the pie immediately with the seasonal vegetables.

Ingredients   SERVES 4

1 onion, peeled and chopped
1 leek, trimmed and chopped
225 ml/8 fl oz chicken stock
3 x 175 g/6 oz chicken breasts
150 ml/$^{1}/_{4}$ pint dry white wine
1 bay leaf
175 g/6 oz baby button mushrooms
2 tbsp plain flour
1 tbsp freshly chopped tarragon
salt and freshly ground black pepper
sprig of fresh parsley, to garnish
seasonal vegetables, to serve

For the topping:

75 g/3 oz (about 5 sheets) filo pastry
1 tbsp sunflower oil
1 tsp sesame seeds

Turkey Escalopes with Apricot Chutney

1 Put a turkey steak onto a sheet of non-pvc clingfilm or non-stick baking parchment. Cover with a second sheet. Using a rolling pin, gently pound the turkey until the meat is flattened to about 5 mm/^{1}/$_4$ inch thick. Repeat to make 4 escalopes.

2 Mix the flour with the salt and pepper and use to lightly dust the turkey escalopes. Put the turkey escalopes on a board or baking tray and cover with a piece of non-pvc clingfilm or non-stick baking parchment. Chill in the refrigerator until ready to cook.

3 For the apricot chutney, put the apricots, onion, ginger, sugar, orange rind, orange juice, port and clove into a saucepan. Slowly bring to the boil and simmer, uncovered, for 10 minutes, stirring occasionally, until thick and syrupy.

4 Remove the clove and stir in the chopped coriander.

5 Heat the oil in a pan and chargriddle the turkey escalopes, in two batches if necessary, for 3–4 minutes on each side until golden brown and tender.

6 Spoon the chutney onto four individual serving plates. Place a turkey escalope on top of each spoonful of chutney. Garnish with sprigs of parsley and serve immediately with orange wedges.

Ingredients   SERVES 4

4 x 175–225 g/6–8 oz turkey steaks
1 tbsp plain flour
salt and freshly ground black pepper
1 tbsp olive oil
flat-leaf parsley sprigs, to garnish
orange wedges, to serve

For the apricot chutney:

125 g/4 oz no-need-to-soak dried
     apricots, chopped
1 red onion, peeled and finely
     chopped
1 tsp fresh root ginger, grated
2 tbsp caster sugar
finely grated rind of ^{1}/$_2$ orange
125 ml/4 fl oz fresh orange juice
125 ml/4 fl oz ruby port
1 whole clove
1 tbsp freshly chopped coriander

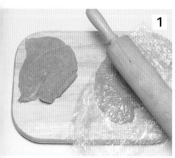

Chicken & White Wine Risotto

1 Heat the oil and half the butter in a large heavy-based saucepan over a medium-high heat. Add the shallots and cook for 2 minutes, or until softened, stirring frequently. Add the rice and cook for 2–3 minutes, stirring frequently, until the rice is translucent and well coated.

2 Pour in half the wine; it will bubble and steam rapidly. Cook, stirring constantly, until the liquid is absorbed. Add a ladleful of the hot stock and cook until the liquid is absorbed. Carefully stir in the chicken.

3 Continue adding the stock, about half a ladleful at a time, allowing each addition to be absorbed before adding the next; never allow the rice to cook dry. This process should take about 20 minutes. The risotto should have a creamy consistency and the rice should be tender, but firm to the bite.

4 Stir in the remaining wine and cook for 2–3 minutes. Remove from the heat and stir in the remaining butter with the Parmesan cheese and half the chopped herbs. Season to taste with salt and pepper. Spoon into warmed shallow bowls and sprinkle each with the remaining chopped herbs. Serve immediately.

Ingredients   SERVES 4–6

2 tbsp oil
125 g/4 oz unsalted butter
2 shallots, peeled and finely chopped
300 g/11 oz Arborio rice
600 ml/1 pint dry white wine
750 ml/1¼ pints chicken
    stock, heated
350 g/12 oz skinless chicken breast
    fillets, thinly sliced
50 g/2 oz Parmesan cheese, grated
2 tbsp freshly chopped dill or parsley
salt and freshly ground black pepper

Helpful hint

Keep the stock to be added to the risotto at a low simmer in a separate saucepan, so that it is piping hot when added to the rice. This will ensure that the dish is kept at a constant heat during cooking, which is important to achieve a perfect creamy texture.

Spinach Dumplings with Rich Tomato Sauce

1 To make the tomato sauce, heat the olive oil in a large saucepan and fry the onion gently for 5 minutes. Add the garlic and chilli and cook for a further 5 minutes, until softened.

2 Stir in the wine, chopped tomatoes and lemon rind. Bring to the boil, cover and simmer for 20 minutes, then uncover and simmer for 15 minutes, or until the sauce has thickened. Remove the lemon rind and season to taste with salt and pepper.

3 To make the spinach dumplings, wash the spinach thoroughly and remove any tough stalks. Cover and cook in a large saucepan over a low heat with just the water clinging to the leaves. Drain, then squeeze out all the excess water. Finely chop and put in a large bowl.

4 Add the ricotta, breadcrumbs, Parmesan cheese and egg yolk to the spinach. Season with nutmeg and salt and pepper. Mix together and shape into 20 walnut-sized balls.

5 Toss the spinach balls in the flour. Heat the olive oil in a large non-stick frying pan and fry the balls gently for 5–6 minutes, carefully turning occasionally. Garnish with fresh basil leaves and serve immediately with the tomato sauce and tagliatelle.

Ingredients   SERVES 4

For the sauce:

2 tbsp olive oil
1 onion, peeled and chopped
1 garlic clove, peeled and crushed
1 red chilli, deseeded and chopped
150 ml/$^1/_4$ pint dry white wine
400 g can chopped tomatoes
pared strip of lemon rind

For the dumplings:

450 g/1 lb fresh spinach
50 g/2 oz ricotta cheese
25 g/1 oz fresh white breadcrumbs
25 g/1 oz Parmesan cheese, grated
1 medium egg yolk
$^1/_4$ tsp freshly grated nutmeg
salt and freshly ground black pepper
5 tbsp plain flour
2 tbsp olive oil, for frying
fresh basil leaves, to garnish
freshly cooked tagliatelle, to serve

Effortless Desserts

These recipes enable you to make mouth-watering desserts in just a few simple steps. From the effortless Fruit Salad to the stunning Passion Fruit and Citrus Tart, it has never been easier to impress your guests, or just indulge yourself.

Poached Pears

1   Place the cinnamon sticks on the work surface and, with a rolling pin, slowly roll down the side of the cinnamon stick to bruise. Place in a large heavy-based saucepan.

2   Add the sugar, wine, water, pared orange rind and juice to the pan and bring slowly to the boil, stirring occasionally, until the sugar is dissolved.

3   Meanwhile, peel the pears, leaving the stalks on.

4   Cut out the cores from the bottom of the pears and level them so that they stand upright.

5   Stand the pears in the syrup, cover the pan and simmer for 20 minutes or until tender.

6   Remove the pan from the heat and leave the pears to cool in the syrup, turning occasionally.

7   Arrange the pears on serving plates and spoon over the syrup. Decorate with the orange slices and serve with the yogurt or low-fat ice cream and any remaining juices.

Ingredients   SERVES 4

2 small cinnamon sticks
125 g/4 oz caster sugar
300 ml/$^1/_2$ pint red wine
150 ml/$^1/_4$ pint water
juice and thinly pared rind
   of 1 small orange
4 firm pears
orange slices, to decorate
frozen vanilla yogurt or low-fat
   ice cream, to serve

Tasty tip

Poached pears are delicious served with a little half-fat crème fraîche and sprinkled with toasted almonds. To toast almonds, simply warm the grill and place whole blanched almonds or flaked almonds on to a piece of foil. Place under the grill and toast lightly on both sides for 1–2 minutes until golden. Remove and cool, chop if liked.

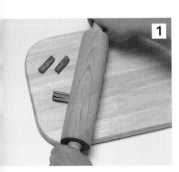

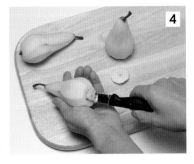

Fruit Salad

1   Place the sugar and 300 ml/¹/₂ pint of water in a small pan and heat, gently stirring, until the sugar has dissolved. Bring to the boil and simmer for 2 minutes. Once a syrup has formed, remove from the heat and allow to cool.

2   Using a sharp knife, cut away the skin from the oranges, then slice thickly. Cut each slice in half and place in a serving dish with the syrup and lychees.

3   Peel the mango, then cut into thick slices around each side of the stone. Discard the stone and cut the slices into bite-size pieces and add to the syrup.

4   Using a sharp knife again, carefully cut away the skin from the pineapple. Remove the central core using the knife or an apple corer, then cut the pineapple into segments and add to the syrup.

6   Peel the papaya, then cut in half and remove the seeds. Cut the flesh into chunks, slice the ginger into matchsticks and add with the ginger syrup to the fruit in the syrup.

7   Prepare the Cape gooseberries by removing the thin, papery skins and rinsing lightly. Add to the syrup.

8   Halve the strawberries, add to the fruit with the essence and chill for 30 minutes. Scatter with mint and lime zest and serve.

Ingredients   SERVES 4

125 g/4 oz caster sugar
3 oranges
700 g/1¹/₂ lb lychees,
    peeled and stoned
1 small mango
1 small pineapple
1 papaya
4 pieces stem ginger in syrup
4 tbsp stem ginger syrup
125 g/4 oz Cape gooseberries
125 g/4 oz strawberries, hulled
¹/₂ tsp almond essence

To decorate:
lime zest
mint leaves

Food fact
A fruit salad is the perfect end to a good meal because it refreshes the palate and is also packed full of vitamins.

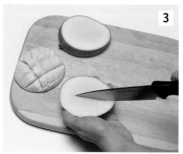

Chocolate Mallow Pie

1 Lightly oil an 18 cm/7 inch flan tin. Place the biscuits in a polythene bag and finely crush with a rolling pin. Alternatively, place in a food processor and blend until fine crumbs are formed.

2 Melt the butter in a medium-sized saucepan, add the crushed biscuits and mix together. Press into the base of the prepared tin and leave to cool in the refrigerator.

3 Melt 125 g/4 oz of the chocolate with the marshmallows and 2 tablespoons of water in a saucepan over a gentle heat, stirring constantly. Leave to cool slightly, then stir in the egg yolk, beat well, then place in the refrigerator until cool.

4 Whisk the egg white until stiff and standing in peaks, then fold into the chocolate mixture.

5 Lightly whip the cream and fold three-quarters of the cream into the chocolate mixture. Reserve the remainder. Spoon the chocolate cream into the flan case and chill in the refrigerator until set.

6 When ready to serve, spoon the remaining cream over the chocolate pie, swirling in a decorative pattern. Grate the remaining dark chocolate and sprinkle over the cream, then serve.

Ingredients SERVES 6

200 g/7 oz digestive biscuits
75 g/3 oz butter, melted
175 g/6 oz plain dark chocolate
20 marshmallows
1 medium egg, separated
300 ml/¹/₂ pint double cream

Tasty tip

Replace the digestive biscuits with an equal weight of chocolate-covered digestive biscuits to make a quick change to this recipe.

Fruity Roulade

1 Preheat the oven to 220°C/425°F/Gas Mark 7. Lightly oil and line a 33 x 23 cm/13 x 9 inch Swiss roll tin with greaseproof paper or baking parchment.

2 Using an electric whisk, whisk the eggs and sugar until the mixture is doubled in volume and leaves a trail across the top.

3 Fold in the flour with a metal spoon or rubber spatula. Pour into the prepared tin and bake in the preheated oven for 10–12 minutes, until well risen and golden.

4 Place a whole sheet of greaseproof paper or baking parchment out on a flat work surface and sprinkle evenly with caster sugar.

5 Turn the cooked sponge out on to the fresh paper, discard the 'cooked' paper, trim the sponge and roll up, encasing the fresh paper inside. Reserve until cool.

6 To make the filling, mix together the Quark, yogurt, caster sugar, liqueur (if using) and orange rind. Unroll the roulade and spread over the mixture. Scatter over the strawberries and roll back up, without the paper this time.

7 Decorate the roulade with the strawberries. Dust with the icing sugar and serve.

Ingredients SERVES 4

For the sponge:
3 medium eggs
75 g/3 oz caster sugar
75 g/3 oz plain flour, sieved
1–2 tbsp caster sugar, for sprinkling

For the filling:
125 g/4 oz Quark
125 g/4 oz half-fat Greek yogurt
25 g/1 oz caster sugar
1 tbsp orange liqueur (optional)
grated rind of 1 orange
125 g/4 oz strawberries, hulled and cut into quarters

To decorate:
strawberries
sifted icing sugar

Food fact
Quark is a soft unripened cheese with the flavour and texture of soured cream. It comes in low-fat and non-fat varieties.

Passion Fruit & Pomegranate Citrus Tart

1 Preheat the oven to 200°C/400°F/Gas Mark 6. Sift the flour and salt into a large bowl and rub in the butter until the mixture resembles fine breadcrumbs. Stir in the sugar.

2 Whisk the egg yolk and add to the dry ingredients. Mix well to form a smooth, pliable dough. Knead gently on a lightly floured surface until smooth. Wrap the pastry and leave to rest in the refrigerator for 30 minutes.

3 Roll out the pastry onto a lightly floured surface and use to line a 25.5 cm/10 inch loose-based flan tin. Line the pastry case with greaseproof paper and baking beans. Brush the edges of the pastry with the egg white and bake blind in the preheated oven for 15 minutes. Remove the paper and beans and bake for 5 minutes. Remove and reduce the temperature to 180°C/350°F/Gas Mark 4.

4 Halve the passion fruit and spoon the flesh into a bowl. Whisk the sugar and eggs together in a bowl. When mixed thoroughly, stir in the double cream with passion fruit juice and flesh and the lime juice.

5 Pour the mixture into the pastry case and bake for 30–40 minutes or until the filling is just set. Remove and cool slightly, then chill in the refrigerator for 1 hour. Cut the pomegranate in half and scoop the seeds into a sieve. Spoon the drained seeds over the top and, just before serving, dust with icing sugar.

Ingredients   SERVES 4

For the pastry:
175 g/6 oz plain flour
pinch of salt
125 g/4 oz butter
4 tsp caster sugar
1 small egg, separated

For the filling:
2 passion fruit
175 g/6 oz caster sugar
4 large eggs
175 ml/6 fl oz double cream
3 tbsp lime juice
1 pomegranate
icing sugar, for dusting

Helpful hint
Pomegranates have leathery skin and may be a dark yellow to a crimson colour. They have a distinctive, slightly acidic flavour.

Chocolate Pecan Angel Pie

1. Preheat the oven to 110°C/225°F/Gas Mark ¼, 5 minutes before baking. Lightly oil a 23 cm/9 inch pie plate. Using an electric mixer, whisk the egg whites and cream of tartar on a low speed until foamy, then increase the speed and beat until soft peaks form. Gradually beat in the sugar, 1 tablespoon at a time, until stiff glossy peaks form and the sugar is completely dissolved. (Test by rubbing a bit of meringue between your fingers – if gritty, continue beating.) This will take about 15 minutes.

2. Beat in 2 teaspoons of the vanilla essence, then fold in the nuts and the chocolate chips. Spread the meringue evenly in the pie plate, making a shallow well in the centre and slightly building up the sides. Bake in the preheated oven for 1–1¼ hours or until a golden creamy colour. Lower the oven temperature if the meringue colours too quickly. Turn the oven off, but do not remove the meringue. Leave the oven door ajar (about 5 cm/2 inches) for about 1 hour. Transfer to a wire rack until cold.

3. Pour the double cream into a small saucepan and bring to the boil. Remove from the heat, add the grated white chocolate and stir until melted. Add the remaining vanilla essence and leave to cool, then whip until thick. Spoon the white chocolate whipped cream into the pie shell, piling it high and swirling decoratively. Decorate with fresh raspberries and chocolate curls. Chill in the refrigerator for 2 hours before serving. When ready to serve, add sprigs of mint on the top and cut into slices.

Ingredients

CUTS INTO 8–10 SLICES

4 large egg whites
¼ tsp cream of tartar
225 g/8 oz caster sugar
3 tsp vanilla essence
100 g/3½ oz pecans, lightly toasted and chopped
75 g/3 oz dark chocolate chips
150 ml/¼ pint double cream
150 g/5 oz white chocolate, grated

To decorate:

fresh raspberries
dark chocolate curls
few sprigs of fresh mint

Helpful hint

The meringue needs to be cooked gently at a low temperature and then allowed to cool in the oven so that it can become crisp and dry without cracking too much.

Frozen Mississippi Mud Pie

1 To make the crust, place the biscuits with the melted butter, sugar and ginger in a food processor and blend together. Press into the sides of a 23 cm/9 inch loose-based flan tin with the back of a spoon and freeze for 30 minutes.

2 Soften the ice creams at room temperature for about 25 minutes. Spoon the chocolate ice cream into the crumb crust, spreading it evenly over the base, then spoon the coffee ice cream over the chocolate ice cream, mounding it slightly in the centre. Return to the freezer to refreeze the ice cream.

3 For the topping, heat the dark chocolate with the cream, golden syrup and vanilla essence in a saucepan. Stir until the chocolate has melted and is smooth. Pour into a bowl and chill in the refrigerator, stirring occasionally, until cold but not set.

4 Spread the cooled chocolate mixture over the top of the frozen pie. Sprinkle with the chocolate and return to the freezer for 1¹/₂ hours or until firm. Serve at room temperature.

Ingredients
CUTS INTO
6–8 SLICES

For the ginger crumb crust:
24–26 gingernut biscuits, crushed
100 g/31/2 oz butter, melted
1–2 tbsp sugar, or to taste
1/2 tsp ground ginger

For the filling:
600 ml/1 pint chocolate ice cream
600 ml/1 pint coffee ice cream

For the chocolate topping:
175 g/6 oz plain dark
   chocolate, chopped
50 ml/2 fl oz single cream
1 tbsp golden syrup
1 tsp vanilla essence
50 g/2 oz coarsely grated white
   and milk chocolate

Helpful hint
Use the best quality ice cream that is available for this recipe. Look for ice cream with added ingredients such as chocolate chips or pieces of toffee.

Crunchy Rhubarb Crumble

1 Preheat the oven to 180°C/350°F/Gas Mark 4. Place the flour in a large bowl and cut the butter into cubes. Add to the flour and rub in with the fingertips until the mixture resembles fine breadcrumbs, or blend for a few seconds in a food processor.

2 Stir in the rolled oats, demerara sugar, sesame seeds and cinnamon. Mix well and reserve.

3 Prepare the rhubarb by removing the thick ends of the stalks and cutting diagonally into 2.5 cm/1 inch chunks. Wash thoroughly and pat dry with a clean tea towel. Place the rhubarb in a 1.1 litre/2 pint pie dish.

4 Sprinkle the caster sugar over the rhubarb and top with the reserved crumble mixture. Level the top of the crumble so that all the fruit is well covered and press down firmly. If liked, sprinkle the top with a little extra caster sugar.

5 Place on a baking sheet and bake in the preheated oven for 40–50 minutes, or until the fruit is soft and the topping is golden brown. Sprinkle the pudding with some more caster sugar and serve hot with custard or cream.

Ingredients SERVES 6

125 g/4 oz plain flour
50 g/2 oz softened butter
50 g/2 oz rolled oats
50 g/2 oz demerara sugar
1 tbsp sesame seeds
$\frac{1}{2}$ tsp ground cinnamon
450 g/1 lb fresh rhubarb
50 g/2 oz caster sugar
custard or cream, to serve

Tasty tip

To make homemade custard, pour 600 ml/1 pint of milk with a few drops of vanilla essence into a saucepan and bring to the boil. Remove from the heat and allow to cool. Meanwhile, whisk 5 egg yolks and 3 tablespoons of caster sugar together in a mixing bowl until thick and pale in colour. Add the milk, stir and strain into a heavy-based saucepan. Cook the custard on a low heat, stirring constantly, until the consistency of double cream. Pour over the rhubarb crumble and serve.

Lattice Treacle Tart

1 Preheat the oven to 190°C/375°F/Gas Mark 5. Make the pastry by placing the flour, butter and white vegetable fat in a food processor. Blend in short sharp bursts until the mixture resembles fine breadcrumbs. Remove from the processor and place onto a pastry board or into a large bowl.

2 Stir in enough cold water to make a dough and knead in a large bowl or on a floured surface until smooth and pliable.

3 Roll out the pastry and use to line a 20.5 cm/8 inch loose-bottomed fluted flan dish or tin. Reserve the pastry trimmings for decoration. Chill for 30 minutes.

4 Meanwhile, to make the filling, place the golden syrup in a saucepan and warm gently with the lemon rind and juice. Tip the breadcrumbs into the pastry case and pour the syrup mixture over the top.

5 Roll the pastry trimmings out onto a lightly floured surface and cut into 6–8 thin strips. Lightly dampen the pastry edge of the tart, then place the strips across the filling in a lattice pattern. Brush the ends of the strips with water and seal to the edge of the tart. Brush a little beaten egg over the pastry and bake in the preheated oven for 25 minutes, or until the filling is just set. Serve hot or cold.

Ingredients   SERVES 4

For the pastry:

175 g/6 oz plain flour
40 g/1½ oz butter
40 g/1½ oz white vegetable fat

For the filling:

225 g/8 oz golden syrup
juice and finely grated rind
   of 1 lemon
75 g/3 oz fresh white breadcrumbs
1 small egg, beaten

Tasty tip

Why not replace the breadcrumbs with the same amount of desiccated coconut?

2

4

5

Chocolate Fruit Pizza

1 Preheat the oven to 200°C/400°F/Gas Mark 6, 15 minutes before baking. Lightly oil a large baking sheet. To make the pastry, place the flour, salt, sugar and cocoa powder in a food processor with the butter and blend briefly. Add the egg yolks, 2 tablespoons of iced water and the vanilla essence and blend until a soft dough is formed. Remove and knead until smooth, wrap in clingfilm and chill for 1 hour. Roll the prepared pastry out to a 23 cm/9 inch round, place the pastry round onto the baking sheet and crimp the edges. Using a fork, prick the base all over and chill in the refrigerator for 30 minutes.

2 Line the pastry with foil and weigh down with an ovenproof flat dinner plate or base of a large flan tin and bake blind in the preheated oven until the edges begin to colour. Remove from the oven and discard the weight and foil. Carefully smooth the chocolate spread over the pizza base and arrange the peach and nectarine slices around the outside edge in overlapping circles. Toss the berries with the plain chocolate and arrange in the centre. Drizzle with the melted butter and sprinkle with the sugar.

3 Bake in the preheated oven for 10–12 minutes, or until the fruit begins to soften. Transfer the pizza to a wire rack. Sprinkle the white chocolate and hazelnuts on top and return to the oven for 1 minute or until the chocolate begins to soften. If the pastry starts to darken too much, cover the edge with strips of foil. Cool on a wire rack. Decorate with fresh mint and serve warm.

Ingredients   SERVES 8

For the sweet chocolate shortcrust pastry:

150 g/5 oz plain flour
½ tsp salt
3–4 tbsp icing sugar
4 tbsp cocoa powder
125 g/4 oz unsalted butter, diced
2 medium egg yolks, beaten
½ tsp vanilla essence

For the topping:

2 tbsp chocolate spread
1 small peach, very thinly sliced
1 small nectarine, very thinly sliced
150 g/5 oz strawberries, halved
   or quartered
75 g/3 oz raspberries
75 g/3 oz blueberries
75 g/3 oz plain dark chocolate,
   coarsely chopped
1 tbsp butter, melted
2 tbsp sugar
75 g/3 oz white chocolate, chopped
1 tbsp hazelnuts, toasted and chopped
sprigs of fresh mint, to decorate

Sweet-stewed Dried Fruits

1 Place the fruits, apple juice, clear honey and brandy in a small saucepan.

2 Using a small, sharp knife or a zester, carefully remove the zest from the lemon and orange and place in the pan.

3 Squeeze the juice from the lemon and orange and add to the pan.

4 Bring the fruit mixture to the boil and simmer for about 1 minute. Remove the pan from the heat and allow the mixture to cool completely.

5 Transfer the mixture to a large bowl, cover with clingfilm and chill in the refrigerator overnight to allow the flavours to blend.

6 Spoon the stewed fruit in to 4 shallow dessert dishes. Decorate with a large spoonful of half-fat crème fraîche and a few strips of the pared orange rind and serve.

Ingredients   SERVES 4

500 g/1 lb 2 oz packet
    mixed dried fruit salad
450 ml/³/₄ pint apple juice
2 tbsp clear honey
2 tbsp brandy
1 lemon
1 orange

To decorate:

half-fat crème fraîche
fine strips of pared orange rind

Tasty tip

As a dessert, this dish is particularly good when served with cold rice pudding. However, these stewed fruits can also be very nice for breakfast. Simply pour some unsweetened muesli into the bottom of a bowl, top with the stewed fruits and perhaps some low-fat natural yogurt and serve.

Baked Stuffed Amaretti Peaches

1 Preheat oven to 180°C/350°F/Gas Mark 4. Halve the peaches and remove the stones. Take a very thin slice from the bottom of each peach half so that it will sit flat on a baking sheet. Dip the peach halves in lemon juice and arrange on the baking sheet.

2 Crush the Amaretti biscuits lightly and put into a large bowl. Add the almonds, pine nuts, sugar, lemon zest and butter. Work with the fingertips until the mixture resembles coarse breadcrumbs. Add the egg yolk and mix well until the mixture is just binding.

3 Divide the Amaretti and nut mixture between the peach halves, pressing down lightly. Bake in the preheated oven for 15 minutes, or until the peaches are tender and the filling is golden. Remove from the oven and drizzle with the honey.

4 Place 2 peach halves on each serving plate and spoon over a little crème fraîche or Greek yogurt, then serve.

Ingredients   SERVES 4

4 ripe peaches
grated zest and juice of 1 lemon
75 g/3 oz Amaretti biscuits
50 g/2 oz chopped, blanched
    almonds, toasted
50 g/2 oz pine nuts, toasted
40 g/1½ oz light muscovado sugar
50 g/2 oz butter
1 medium egg yolk
2 tsp clear honey
crème fraîche or Greek yogurt,
    to serve

Tasty tip

If fresh peaches are unavailable, use nectarines. Alternatively, use drained, tinned peach halves that have been packed in juice, rather than syrup. You can vary the filling according to personal preference – try ground almonds, caster sugar, crumbled trifle sponge cakes and lemon rind, moistened with medium sherry.

Fruity Chocolate Bread Pudding

1 Preheat the oven to 180°C/350°F/Gas Mark 4, 10 minutes before cooking. Lightly butter a shallow ovenproof dish. Break the chocolate into small pieces, then place in a heatproof bowl set over a saucepan of gently simmering water. Heat gently, stirring frequently, until the chocolate has melted and is smooth. Remove from the heat and leave for about 10 minutes or until the chocolate begins to thicken slightly.

2 Cut the fruit loaf into medium to thick slices, then spread with the melted chocolate. Leave until almost set, then cut each slice in half to form a triangle. Layer the chocolate-coated bread slices and the chopped apricots in the buttered ovenproof dish.

3 Stir the cream and the milk together, then stir in the caster sugar. Beat the eggs, then gradually beat into the cream and milk mixture. Beat thoroughly until well blended. Carefully pour over the bread slices and apricots and leave to stand for 30 minutes.

4 Sprinkle with the demerara sugar and place in a roasting tin half filled with boiling water. Cook in the preheated oven for 45 minutes, or until golden and the custard is lightly set. Serve immediately.

Ingredients   SERVES 4

175 g/6 oz plain dark chocolate
1 small fruit loaf
125 g/4 oz ready-to-eat dried
    apricots, roughly chopped
450 ml/³/₄ pint single cream
300 ml/¹/₂ pint milk
1 tbsp caster sugar
3 medium eggs
3 tbsp demerara sugar, for sprinkling

Helpful hint

It is important to leave the pudding to stand for at least 30 minutes, as described in step 3. This allows the custard to soak into the bread – otherwise it sets around the bread as it cooks, making the pudding seem stodgy.

Chocolate & Fruit Crumble

1 Preheat the oven to 190°C/375°F/Gas Mark 5, 10 minutes before baking. Lightly oil an ovenproof dish.

2 For the crumble, sift the flour into a large bowl. Cut the butter into small dice and add to the flour. Rub the butter into the flour until the mixture resembles fine breadcrumbs.

3 Stir the sugar, porridge oats and chopped hazelnuts into the mixture and reserve.

4 For the filling, peel the apples, core and slice thickly. Place in a large heavy-based saucepan with the lemon juice and 3 tablespoons of water. Add the sultanas, raisins and soft brown sugar. Bring slowly to the boil, cover and simmer over a gentle heat for 8–10 minutes, stirring occasionally, or until the apples are slightly softened.

5 Remove the saucepan from the heat and leave to cool slightly before stirring in the pears, ground cinnamon and chopped chocolate.

6 Spoon into the prepared ovenproof dish. Sprinkle the crumble evenly over the top, then bake in the preheated oven for 35–40 minutes, or until the top is golden. Remove from the oven, sprinkle with the caster sugar and serve immediately.

Ingredients   SERVES 4

For the crumble:
125 g/4 oz plain flour
125 g/4 oz butter
75 g/3 oz light soft brown sugar
50 g/2 oz rolled porridge oats
50 g/2 oz hazelnuts, chopped

For the filling:
450 g/1 lb Bramley apples
1 tbsp lemon juice
50 g/2 oz sultanas
50 g/2 oz seedless raisins
50 g/2 oz light soft brown sugar
350 g/12 oz pears, peeled,
    cored and chopped
1 tsp ground cinnamon
125 g/4 oz plain dark chocolate,
    very roughly chopped
2 tsp caster sugar, for sprinkling

Tasty tip
Bramley apples are ideal for cooking and will purée very easily. If you prefer, use a dessert apple such as Golden Delicious, but reduce the sugar accordingly.

Osborne Pudding

1 Preheat the oven to 170°C/325°F/Gas Mark 3. Lightly oil a 1.1 litre/2 pint baking dish.

2 Remove the crusts from the bread and spread thickly with the butter and marmalade. Cut the bread into small triangles.

3 Place half the bread in the base of the dish and sprinkle over the dried mixed fruit, 1 tablespoon of the orange juice and half the caster sugar. Top with the remaining bread and marmalade, buttered side up and pour over the remaining orange juice. Sprinkle over the remaining caster sugar.

4 Whisk the eggs with the milk and cream and pour over the pudding. Reserve for about 30 minutes to allow the bread to absorb the liquid. Place in a roasting tin and pour in enough boiling water to come halfway up the sides of the dish. Bake in the preheated oven for 50–60 minutes, or until the pudding is set and the top is crisp and golden.

5 Meanwhile, make the marmalade sauce. Heat the orange zest and juice with the marmalade and brandy, if using. Mix 1 tablespoon of water with the cornflour and mix together well. Add to the saucepan and cook on a low heat, stirring until warmed through and thickened. Serve the pudding hot with the marmalade sauce.

Ingredients   SERVES 4

8 slices of white bread
50 g/2 oz butter
2 tbsp marmalade
50 g/2 oz luxury mixed dried fruit
2 tbsp fresh orange juice
40 g/1½ oz caster sugar
2 large eggs
450 ml/¾ pint milk
150 ml/¼ pint whipping cream

For the marmalade sauce:

zest and juice of 1 orange
2 tbsp thick-cut orange marmalade
1 tbsp brandy (optional)
2 tsp cornflour

Tasty tip

To make an orange sauce instead, omit the marmalade and add the juice of another 3 oranges and a squeeze of lemon juice to make 250 ml/9 fl oz. Follow the recipe as before but increase the cornflour to 1½ tablespoons.

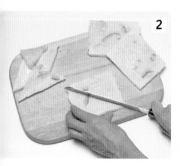

Mocha Pie

1   Place the prepared pastry case onto a large serving plate and reserve. Melt the chocolate in a heatproof bowl set over a saucepan of simmering water. Ensure the water is not touching the base of the bowl. Remove from the heat, stir until smooth and leave to cool.

2   Cream the butter, soft brown sugar and vanilla essence until light and fluffy, then beat in the cooled chocolate. Add the strong black coffee, pour into the pastry case and chill in the refrigerator for about 30 minutes.

3   For the topping, whisk the cream until beginning to thicken, then whisk in the sugar and vanilla essence. Continue to whisk until the cream is softly peaking. Spoon just under half the cream into a separate bowl and fold in the dissolved coffee.

4   Spread the remaining cream over the filling in the pastry case. Spoon the coffee-flavoured whipped cream evenly over the top, then swirl it decoratively with a palate knife. Sprinkle with grated chocolate and chill in the refrigerator until ready to serve.

Ingredients   SERVES 4–6

1 x 23 cm/9 inch ready-made
   sweet pastry case

For the filling:

125 g/4 oz plain dark chocolate,
   broken into pieces
175 g/6 oz unsalted butter
225 g/8 oz soft brown sugar
1 tsp vanilla essence
3 tbsp strong black coffee

For the topping:

600 ml/1 pint double cream
50 g/2 oz icing sugar
2 tsp vanilla essence
1 tsp instant coffee dissolved in
   1 tsp boiling water and cooled
grated plain and white chocolate,
   to decorate

Helpful hint

Using a ready-made pastry case makes this a quickly made store cupboard pie that looks very impressive.

Spicy White Chocolate Mousse

1 Tap the cardamom pods lightly so they split. Remove the seeds, then, using a pestle and mortar, crush lightly. Pour the milk into a small saucepan and add the crushed seeds and the bay leaves. Bring to the boil gently over a medium heat. Remove from the heat, cover and leave in a warm place for at least 30 minutes to infuse.

2 Break the chocolate into small pieces and place in a heatproof bowl set over a saucepan of gently simmering water. Ensure the water is not touching the base of the bowl. When the chocolate has melted, remove the bowl from the heat and stir until smooth.

3 Whip the cream until it has slightly thickened and holds its shape, but does not form peaks. Reserve. Whisk the egg whites in a clean, grease-free bowl until stiff and standing in soft peaks.

4 Strain the milk through a sieve into the cooled, melted chocolate and beat until smooth. Spoon the chocolate mixture into the egg whites, then, using a large metal spoon, fold gently. Add the whipped cream and fold in gently.

5 Spoon into a large serving dish or individual small cups. Chill in the refrigerator for 3–4 hours. Just before serving, dust with a little sifted cocoa powder and then serve.

Ingredients   SERVES 4–6

6 cardamom pods
125 ml/4 fl oz milk
3 bay leaves
200 g/7 oz white chocolate
300 ml/$^1/_2$ pint double cream
3 medium egg whites
1–2 tsp cocoa powder, sifted,
  for dusting

Tasty tip
Chocolate and spices go together very well as this recipe demonstrates. White chocolate has an affinity with spices such as cardamom, while dark and milk chocolate go very well with cinnamon.

Entertaining

Now that you have mastered the basics, try these simple-to-follow yet sophisticated dishes that will amaze your guests. The range of recipes helps you to cater for every occasion and for whatever your guests need with nibbles, fish courses, vegetarian and meat dishes.

Mixed Canapés

1 For the cheese canapés, cut the crusts off the bread, then gently roll with a rolling pin to flatten slightly. Thinly spread with butter, then sprinkle over the mixed cheeses as evenly as possible.

2 Roll up each slice tightly, then cut into 4 slices, each about 2.5 cm/1 inch long. Heat the oil in a wok or large frying pan and stir-fry the cheese rolls in 2 batches, turning them all the time until golden brown and crisp. Drain on absorbent kitchen paper and serve warm or cold.

3 For the spicy nuts, melt the butter and oil in a wok, then add the nuts and stir-fry over a low heat for about 5 minutes, stirring all the time, or until they begin to colour.

4 Sprinkle the paprika and cumin over the nuts and continue stir-frying for a further 1–2 minutes, or until the nuts are golden brown.

5 Remove from the wok and drain on absorbent kitchen paper. Sprinkle with the salt, garnish with sprigs of fresh coriander and serve hot or cold. If serving cold, store both the cheese canapés and the spicy nuts in airtight containers.

Ingredients   SERVES 12

For the stir-fried cheese canapés:

6 thick slices white bread
40 g/1½ oz butter, softened
75 g/3 oz mature Cheddar
   cheese, grated
75 g/3 oz blue cheese such as Stilton
   or Gorgonzola, crumbled
3 tbsp sunflower oil

For the spicy nuts:

25 g/1 oz unsalted butter
2 tbsp light olive oil
450 g/1 lb mixed unsalted nuts
1 tsp ground paprika
½ tsp ground cumin
½ tsp fine sea salt
sprigs of fresh coriander, to garnish

Tasty tip

These canapés are perfect for serving at a buffet or finger food party, or you can halve the quantities and serve with drinks instead of a starter at an informal dinner party for 4–6 people.

Potato Pancakes with Smoked Salmon

1 Cook the potatoes in a saucepan of lightly salted boiling water for 15–20 minutes, or until tender. Drain thoroughly, then mash until free of lumps. Beat in the whole egg and egg yolk, together with the butter. Beat until smooth and creamy. Slowly beat in the flour and cream, then season to taste with salt and pepper. Stir in the chopped parsley.

2 Beat the crème fraîche and horseradish sauce together in a small bowl, cover with clingfilm and reserve.

3 Heat a lightly oiled, heavy-based frying pan over a medium-high heat. Place a few spoonfuls of the potato mixture in the hot pan and cook for 4–5 minutes, or until cooked and golden, turning halfway through the cooking time. Remove from the pan, drain on absorbent kitchen paper and keep warm. Repeat with the remaining mixture.

4 Arrange the pancakes on individual serving plates. Place the smoked salmon onto the pancakes and spoon over a little of the horseradish sauce. Serve with salad and the remaining horseradish sauce and garnish with lemon slices and chives.

Ingredients   SERVES 4

450 g/1 lb floury potatoes,
    peeled and quartered
salt and freshly ground black pepper
1 large egg
1 large egg yolk
25 g/1 oz butter
25 g/1 oz plain flour
150 ml/¼ pint double cream
2 tbsp freshly chopped parsley
5 tbsp crème fraîche
1 tbsp horseradish sauce
225 g/8 oz smoked salmon, sliced
salad leaves, to serve

To garnish:
lemon slices
snipped chives

Tasty tip
Horseradish is a pungent root, usually grated and mixed with oil and vinegar or cream to make horseradish sauce. Sauces vary in heat, so it is best to add a little at a time and taste until you have the desired flavour.

Thai Crab Cakes

1 Place the crab meat in a bowl with the ground coriander, chilli, turmeric, lime juice, sugar, ginger, chopped coriander, lemon grass, flour and egg yolks. Mix together well.

2 Divide the mixture into 12 equal portions and form each into a small patty about 5 cm/2 inches across. Lightly whisk the egg whites and put into a dish. Place the breadcrumbs onto a separate plate.

3 Dip each crab cake first in the egg whites, then in the breadcrumbs, turning to coat both sides. Place on a plate, cover and chill in the refrigerator until ready to cook.

4 Heat the oil in a large frying pan. Add 6 crab cakes and cook for 3 minutes on each side, or until crisp and golden brown on the outside and cooked through. Remove, drain on absorbent kitchen paper and keep warm while cooking the remaining cakes. Arrange on plates, garnish with lime wedges and serve immediately with salad leaves.

Ingredients   SERVES 6

225 g/8 oz white and brown crab meat (about equivalent to the flesh of 2 medium crabs)

1 tsp ground coriander

$1/_4$ tsp chilli powder

$1/_4$ tsp ground turmeric

2 tsp lime juice

1 tsp soft light brown sugar

2.5 cm/1 inch piece fresh root ginger, peeled and grated

3 tbsp freshly chopped coriander

2 tsp finely chopped lemon grass

2 tbsp plain flour

2 medium eggs, separated

50 g/2 oz fresh white breadcrumbs

3 tbsp groundnut oil

lime wedges, to garnish

mixed salad leaves, to serve

Sesame Prawn Toasts

1 Place the prawns in a food processor or blender with the cornflour, spring onions, ginger, soy sauce and Chinese five-spice powder, if using. Blend to a fairly smooth paste. Spoon into a bowl and stir in the beaten egg. Season to taste with salt and pepper.

2 Cut the crusts off the bread. Spread the prawn paste in an even layer on one side of each slice. Sprinkle over the sesame seeds and press down lightly.

3 Cut each slice diagonally into 4 triangles. Place on a board and chill in the refrigerator for 30 minutes.

4 Pour sufficient oil into a heavy-based saucepan or deep-fat fryer so that it is one-third full. Heat until it reaches a temperature of 180°C/350°F. Cook the toasts in batches of 5 or 6, carefully lowering them seeded-side down into the oil. Deep-fry for 2–3 minutes, or until lightly browned, then turn over and cook for 1 minute more. Using a slotted spoon, lift out the toasts and drain on absorbent kitchen paper. Keep warm while frying the remaining toasts. Arrange on a warmed platter and serve immediately with some chilli sauce for dipping.

Ingredients   SERVES 4

125 g/4 oz peeled cooked prawns
1 tbsp cornflour
2 spring onions, peeled and
    roughly chopped
2 tsp freshly grated root ginger
2 tsp dark soy sauce
pinch of Chinese five-spice
    powder (optional)
1 small egg, beaten
salt and freshly ground black pepper
6 thin slices day-old white bread
40 g/1^1/$_2$ oz sesame seeds
vegetable oil, for deep-frying
chilli sauce, to serve

Helpful hint

The toasts can be prepared to the end of step 3 up to 12 hours in advance. Cover and chill in the refrigerator until needed. It is important to use bread that is a day or two old and not fresh bread. Make sure that the prawns are well drained before puréeing – pat them dry on absorbent kitchen paper, if necessary.

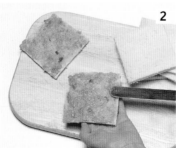
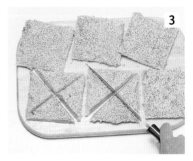

Cooked Vegetable Salad with Satay Sauce

1 Heat a wok, add the oil and, when hot, add the peanuts and stir-fry for 3–4 minutes. Drain on absorbent kitchen paper and leave to cool. Blend in a food processor to a fine powder.

2 Place the onion and garlic, with the spices, sugar, soy sauce, lemon juice and olive oil in a food processor. Season to taste with salt and pepper, then process into a paste. Transfer to a wok and stir-fry for 3–4 minutes.

3 Stir 600 ml/1 pint hot water into the paste and bring to the boil. Add the ground peanuts and simmer gently for 5–6 minutes, or until the mixture thickens. Reserve the satay sauce.

4 Cook the vegetables in batches in lightly salted boiling water: cook the French beans, carrots, cauliflower and broccoli for 3–4 minutes and the Chinese leaves or pak choi and bean sprouts for 2 minutes. Drain each batch, drizzle over the sesame oil and arrange on a large warmed serving dish. Garnish with watercress sprigs and cucumber. Serve with the satay sauce.

Ingredients   SERVES 4

125 ml/4 fl oz groundnut oil
225 g/8 oz unsalted peanuts
1 onion, peeled and finely chopped
1 garlic clove, peeled and crushed
$\frac{1}{2}$ tsp chilli powder
1 tsp ground coriander
$\frac{1}{2}$ tsp ground cumin
$\frac{1}{2}$ tsp sugar
1 tbsp dark soy sauce
2 tbsp fresh lemon juice
2 tbsp light olive oil
salt and freshly ground black pepper
125 g/4 oz French green beans, trimmed and halved
125 g/4 oz carrots
125 g/4 oz cauliflower florets
125 g/4 oz broccoli florets
125 g/4 oz Chinese leaves or pak choi, trimmed and shredded
125 g/4 oz bean sprouts
1 tbsp sesame oil

To garnish:

sprigs of fresh watercress
cucumber, cut into slivers

Mushroom & Red Wine Pâté

1   Preheat the oven to 180°C/350°F/Gas Mark 4. Cut the bread in half diagonally. Place the bread triangles on a baking tray and cook for 10 minutes.

2   Remove from the oven and split each bread triangle in half to make 12 triangles and return to the oven until golden and crisp. Leave to cool on a wire rack.

3   Heat the oil in a saucepan and gently cook the onion and garlic until transparent.

4   Add the mushrooms and cook, stirring, for 3–4 minutes, or until the mushroom juices start to run.

5   Stir the wine and herbs into the mushroom mixture and bring to the boil. Reduce the heat and simmer, uncovered, until all the liquid is absorbed.

6   Remove from the heat and season to taste with salt and pepper. Leave to cool.

7   When cold, beat in the soft cream cheese and adjust the seasoning. Place in a small clean bowl and chill until required. Serve the toast triangles with the cucumber and tomato.

Ingredients   SERVES 4

3 large slices of white bread,
    crusts removed
2 tsp oil
1 small onion, peeled and
    finely chopped
1 garlic clove, peeled and crushed
350 g/12 oz button mushrooms,
    wiped and finely chopped
150 ml/^{1}/$_4$ pint red wine
^{1}/$_2$ tsp dried mixed herbs
1 tbsp freshly chopped parsley
salt and freshly ground black pepper
2 tbsp low-fat cream cheese

To serve:
finely chopped cucumber
finely chopped tomato

Tasty tip
This pâté is also delicious served as a bruschetta topping. Toast slices of ciabatta, spread the pâté generously on top and garnish with a little rocket.

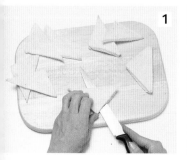

Spicy Prawns in Lettuce Cups

1 Remove 3 or 4 of the tougher outer leaves of the lemon grass and reserve for another dish. Finely chop the remaining softer centre. Place 2 teaspoons of the chopped lemon grass in a bowl with the prawns, grated lime zest, chilli and ginger. Mix together to coat the prawns. Cover and place in the refrigerator to marinate while you make the coconut sauce.

2 For the sauce, place the grated coconut in a wok or nonstick frying pan and dry-fry for 2–3 minutes, or until golden. Remove from the pan and reserve. Add the hoisin, soy and fish sauces to the pan with the sugar and 4 tablespoons of water. Simmer for 2–3 minutes, then remove from the heat. Leave to cool.

3 Pour the sauce over the prawns, add the toasted coconut and toss to mix together. Divide the prawn and coconut sauce mixture between the lettuce leaves and arrange on a platter.

4 Sprinkle over the chopped roasted peanuts and spring onions and garnish with a sprig of fresh coriander. Serve immediately.

Ingredients   SERVES 4

1 lemon grass stalk
225 g/8 oz peeled cooked prawns
1 tsp finely grated lime zest
1 red bird's-eye chilli, deseeded and
  finely chopped
2.5 cm/1 inch piece fresh root
  ginger, peeled and grated
2 Little Gem lettuces, divided
  into leaves
25 g/1 oz roasted peanuts, chopped
2 spring onions, trimmed and
  diagonally sliced
sprig of fresh coriander, to garnish

For the coconut sauce:

2 tbsp freshly grated or unsweetened
  shredded coconut
1 tbsp hoisin sauce
1 tbsp light soy sauce
1 tbsp Thai fish sauce
1 tbsp palm sugar or soft light
  brown sugar

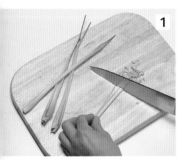

Barbecued Fish Kebabs

1 If using wooden skewers, soak in cold water for 30 minutes to prevent them from catching light during cooking.

2 Meanwhile, prepare the sauce. Add the fish stock, tomato ketchup, Worcestershire sauce, vinegar, sugar, Tabasco and tomato purée to a small saucepan. Stir well and leave to simmer for 5 minutes.

3 Line a grill rack with a single layer of foil and preheat the grill at a high temperature, 2 minutes before use.

4 When ready to cook, drain the skewers, if necessary, then thread the fish chunks, the quartered red onions and the cherry tomatoes alternately onto the skewers.

5 Season the kebabs to taste with salt and pepper and brush with the sauce. Grill under the preheated grill for 8–10 minutes, basting with the sauce occasionally during cooking. Turn the kebabs often to ensure that they are cooked thoroughly and evenly on all sides. Serve immediately with couscous.

Ingredients   SERVES 4

450 g/1 lb herring or mackerel fillets, cut into chunks
2 small red onions, peeled and quartered
16 cherry tomatoes
salt and freshly ground black pepper

For the sauce:

150 ml/¼ pint fish stock
5 tbsp tomato ketchup
2 tbsp Worcestershire sauce
2 tbsp wine vinegar
2 tbsp brown sugar
2 drops Tabasco sauce
2 tbsp tomato purée

Tasty tip

Instead of cooking indoors, cook these kebabs on the barbecue for a delicious charcoaled flavour. Light the barbecue at least 20 minutes before use in order to allow the coals to heat up. Barbecue some peppers and red onions and serve with a mixed salad as an accompaniment to the fish kebabs.

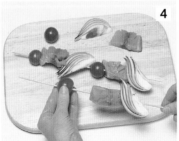

Fish Puff Tart

1 Preheat the oven to 220 C/425 F/Gas Mark 7. On a lightly floured surface, roll out the pastry into a 20.5 x 25.5 cm/8 x 10 inch rectangle.

2 Draw an 18 x 23 cm/7 x 9 inch rectangle in the centre of the pastry, to form a 2.5 cm/1 inch border. (Be careful not to cut through the pastry.)

3 Lightly cut criss-cross patterns in the border of the pastry with a knife.

4 Place the fish on a chopping board and, with a sharp knife, skin the cod and smoked haddock. Cut into thin slices.

5 Spread the pesto evenly over the bottom of the pastry case with the back of a spoon.

6 Arrange the fish, tomatoes and cheese in the pastry case and brush the pastry with the beaten egg.

7 Bake the tart in the preheated oven for 20–25 minutes, until the pastry is well risen, puffed and golden brown. Garnish with the chopped parsley and serve immediately.

Ingredients SERVES 4

350 g/12 oz prepared puff pastry, thawed if frozen
150 g/5 oz smoked haddock
150 g/5 oz cod
1 tbsp pesto
2 tomatoes, sliced
125 g/4 oz goats' cheese, sliced
1 medium egg, beaten
freshly chopped parsley, to garnish

Food fact

The Scottish name for smoked haddock is finnan haddie, named after the Scottish fishing village of Findon near Aberdeen. Smoked haddock has been a favourite breakfast dish in Findon and the rest of Scotland for many years. Although this type of fish was traditionally caught and smoked (sometimes over peat fires) in Scotland, nowadays the fish is produced in New England and other eastern coastal states of the United States.

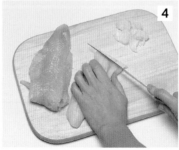

Saffron Roast Chicken with Crispy Onions

1 Preheat the oven to 200°C/400°F/Gas Mark 6. Using your fingertips, gently loosen the skin from the chicken breast by sliding your hand between the skin and flesh. Cream together 50 g/2 oz of the butter with the saffron threads, the lemon rind and half the parsley, until smooth. Push the butter under the skin. Spread over the breast and the tops of the thighs with your fingers. Pull the neck skin to tighten the skin over the breast and tuck under the bird, then secure with a skewer or cocktail stick.

2 Heat the olive oil and remaining butter in a large heavy-based frying pan and cook the onions and garlic cloves for 5 minutes, or until the onions are soft. Stir in the cumin seeds, cinnamon, pine nuts and sultanas and cook for 2 minutes. Season to taste with salt and pepper and place in a roasting tin.

3 Place the chicken, breast-side down, on the base of the onions and roast in the preheated oven for 45 minutes. Reduce the oven temperature to 170°C/325°F/Gas Mark 3. Turn the chicken breast-side up and stir the onions. Continue roasting until the chicken is a deep golden yellow and the onions are crisp. Allow to rest for 10 minutes, then sprinkle with the remaining parsley. Before serving, garnish with a sprig of parsley and serve immediately with the onions and garlic.

Ingredients   SERVES 4–6

1.6 kg/3½ lb oven-ready chicken,
   preferably free range
75 g/3 oz butter, softened
1 tsp saffron strands, lightly toasted
grated rind of 1 lemon
2 tbsp freshly chopped
   flat-leaf parsley
2 tbsp extra virgin olive oil
450 g/1 lb onions, peeled and cut
   into thin wedges
8–12 garlic cloves, peeled
1 tsp cumin seeds
½ tsp ground cinnamon
50 g/2 oz pine nuts
50 g/2 oz sultanas
salt and freshly ground black pepper
sprig of fresh flat-leaf parsley,
   to garnish

Helpful hint

Roasting the chicken breast-side down first helps to ensure that the white meat will be moist. Turning the chicken halfway through cooking will give a crisp, golden skin.

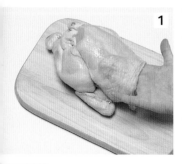

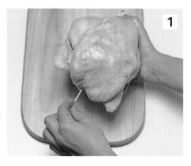

Chicken & New Potatoes on Rosemary Skewers

1 Preheat the grill and line the grill rack with foil just before cooking. Strip the leaves from the rosemary stems, leaving about 5 cm/2 inches of soft leaves at the top. Chop the leaves coarsely and reserve. Using a sharp knife, cut the thicker woody ends of the stems to a point which can pierce the chicken pieces and potatoes. Blend the chopped rosemary, oil, garlic, thyme and lemon rind and juice in a shallow dish. Season to taste with salt and pepper.

2 Cut the chicken into 4 cm/1½ inch cubes, add to the flavoured oil and stir well. Cover, refrigerate for at least 30 minutes, turning occasionally.

3 Cook the potatoes in lightly salted boiling water for 10–12 minutes until just tender. Add the onions to the potatoes 2 minutes before the end of the cooking time. Drain, rinse under cold water and leave to cool. Cut the pepper into 2.5 cm/1 inch squares.

4 Beginning with a piece of chicken and starting with the pointed end of the skewer, alternately thread equal amounts of chicken, potato, pepper and onion onto each rosemary skewer. Cover the leafy ends of the skewers with foil to stop them from burning. Do not thread the chicken and vegetables too closely together on the skewer or the chicken may not cook completely. Cook the kebabs for 15 minutes, or until tender and golden, turning and brushing with either extra oil or the marinade. Remove the foil, garnish with lemon wedges and serve on rice.

Ingredients   SERVES 4

8 thick fresh rosemary stems, at least
    23 cm/9 inches long
3–4 tbsp extra virgin olive oil
2 garlic cloves, peeled and crushed
1 tsp freshly chopped thyme
juice and grated rind of 1 lemon
salt and freshly ground black pepper
4 skinless chicken breast fillets
16 small new potatoes,
    peeled or scrubbed
8 very small onions or
    shallots, peeled
1 large yellow or red
    pepper, deseeded
lemon wedges, to garnish
parsley-flavoured cooked rice,
    to serve

Helpful hint

If using a barbecue, light at least 20 minutes before required.

Sweet-&-Sour Rice with Chicken

1 Trim the spring onions, then cut lengthways into fine strips. Drop into a large bowl of iced water and reserve.

2 Mix together the sesame oil and Chinese five-spice powder and use to rub into the cubed chicken. Heat the wok, then add the oil and, when hot, cook the garlic and onion for 2–3 minutes, or until transparent and softened.

3 Add the chicken and stir-fry over a medium-high heat until the chicken is golden and cooked through. Using a slotted spoon, remove from the wok and keep warm.

4 Stir the rice into the wok and add the water, tomato ketchup, tomato purée, honey, vinegar and soy sauce. Stir well to mix. Bring to the boil, then simmer until almost all of the liquid is absorbed. Stir in the carrot and reserved chicken and continue to cook for 3–4 minutes.

5 Drain the spring onions, which will have become curly. Garnish the rice and chicken with the spring onion curls and serve immediately.

Ingredients
SERVES 4

4 spring onions
2 tsp sesame oil
1 tsp Chinese five-spice powder
450 g/1 lb chicken breast, cut into cubes
1 tbsp oil
1 garlic clove, peeled and crushed
1 medium onion, peeled and sliced
   into thin wedges
225 g/8 oz long-grain white rice
600 ml/1 pint water
4 tbsp tomato ketchup
1 tbsp tomato purée
2 tbsp honey
1 tbsp vinegar
1 tbsp dark soy sauce
1 carrot, peeled and cut into
   matchsticks

Food fact

Five-spice powder is a popular Chinese seasoning that can be bought ready-blended in jars. It is a mixture of finely ground star anise, fennel, cinnamon, cloves and Szechuan pepper and adds a unique aniseed flavour to food.

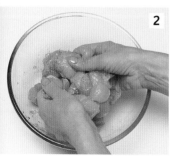

Pad Thai

1 To make the sauce, whisk all the sauce ingredients in a bowl and reserve. Put the rice noodles in a large bowl and pour over enough hot water to cover. Leave to stand for about 15 minutes until softened. Drain and rinse, then drain again.

2 Heat the oil in a wok over a high heat until hot, but not smoking. Add the chicken strips and stir-fry constantly until they begin to colour. Using a slotted spoon, transfer to a plate. Reduce the heat to medium-high.

3 Add the shallots, garlic and spring onions and stir-fry for 1 minute. Stir in the rice noodles, then the reserved sauce; mix well.

4 Add the reserved chicken strips, with the crab meat or prawns, bean sprouts and radish and stir well. Cook for about 5 minutes, stirring frequently, until heated through. If the noodles begin to stick, add a little water.

5 Turn into a large shallow serving dish and sprinkle with the chopped peanuts, if desired. Serve immediately.

Ingredients SERVES 4

225 g/8 oz flat rice noodles
2 tbsp vegetable oil
225 g/8 oz boneless chicken breast,
    skinned and thinly sliced
4 shallots, peeled and thinly sliced
2 garlic cloves, peeled and
    finely chopped
4 spring onions, trimmed and diagonally
    cut into 5 cm/2 inch pieces
350 g/12 oz fresh white crab meat or
    tiny prawns
75 g/3 oz fresh bean sprouts, rinsed
    and drained
2 tbsp preserved or fresh
    radish, chopped
2–3 tbsp roasted peanuts,
    chopped (optional)

For the sauce:

3 tbsp Thai fish sauce (nam pla)
2–3 tbsp rice vinegar or cider vinegar
1 tbsp chilli bean or oyster sauce
1 tbsp toasted sesame oil
1 tbsp light brown sugar
1 red chilli, deseeded and thinly sliced

Turkey & Pesto Rice Roulades

1 Put the rice in a bowl and add the garlic, Parmesan cheese, pesto and pine nuts. Stir to combine the ingredients, then reserve.

2 Place the turkey steaks on a chopping board and, using a sharp knife, cut horizontally through each steak, without cutting right through. Open up the steaks and cover with baking parchment. Flatten slightly by pounding with a meat mallet or rolling pin.

3 Season each steak with salt and pepper. Divide the stuffing equally among the steaks, spreading evenly over one half. Fold the steaks in half to enclose the filling, then wrap each steak in a slice of Parma ham and secure with cocktail sticks.

4 Heat the oil in a large frying pan over a medium heat. Cook the steaks for 5 minutes, or until golden on one side. Turn and cook for a further 2 minutes. Push the steaks to the side and pour in the wine. Allow the wine to bubble and evaporate. Add the butter, a little at a time, whisking constantly until the sauce is smooth. Discard the cocktail sticks, then serve the steaks drizzled with the sauce and serve with spinach and pasta.

Ingredients   SERVES 4

125 g/4 oz cooked white rice,
    at room temperature
1 garlic clove, peeled and crushed
1–2 tbsp Parmesan cheese, grated
2 tbsp prepared pesto
2 tbsp pine nuts, lightly toasted
    and chopped
4 turkey steaks, each weighing
    about 150 g/5 oz
salt and freshly ground black pepper
4 slices Parma ham
2 tbsp olive oil
50 ml/2 fl oz white wine
25 g/1 oz unsalted butter, chilled

To serve:
freshly cooked spinach
freshly cooked pasta

Food fact
The classic Italian Parma ham is dry-cured, whereby it is rubbed with salt for about a month, then hung up to dry for a year. Carved very thinly, it is often served raw, but is also good when lightly fried.

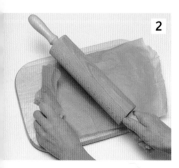

Shredded Duck in Lettuce Leaves

1 Cover the dried Chinese mushrooms with almost-boiling water, leave for 20 minutes, then drain and slice thinly.

2 Heat a large wok, add the oil and, when hot, stir-fry the duck for 3–4 minutes, or until sealed. Remove with a slotted spoon and reserve.

3 Add the chilli, spring onions, garlic and Chinese mushrooms to the wok and stir-fry for 2–3 minutes, or until softened.

4 Add the bean sprouts, soy sauce, Chinese rice wine or dry sherry and honey or brown sugar to the wok and continue to stir-fry for 1 minute, or until blended.

5 Stir in the reserved duck and stir-fry for 2 minutes, or until well mixed together and heated right through. Transfer to a heated serving dish.

6 Arrange the hoisin sauce in a small bowl on a tray or plate with a pile of lettuce leaves and the mint leaves.

7 Let each guest spoon a little hoisin sauce onto a lettuce leaf, then top with a large spoonful of the stir-fried duck and vegetables and roll up the leaf to enclose the filling. Serve with the dipping sauce.

Ingredients   SERVES 4–6

15 g/½ oz dried Chinese (shiitake) mushrooms
2 tbsp vegetable oil
400 g/14 oz boneless, skinless duck breast, cut crossways into thin strips
1 red chilli, deseeded and thinly sliced diagonally
4–6 spring onions, trimmed and diagonally sliced
2 garlic cloves, peeled and crushed
75 g/3 oz bean sprouts
3 tbsp soy sauce
1 tbsp Chinese rice wine or dry sherry
1–2 tsp clear honey or brown sugar
4–6 tbsp hoisin sauce
large, crisp lettuce leaves such as iceberg or cos
handful fresh mint leaves
dipping sauce, to serve

Food fact

Hoisin sauce is a sweet and spicy aromatic Chinese sauce made primarily from soy beans, sugar, garlic and chilli.

Duck with Berry Sauce

1 Remove the skins from the duck breasts and season with a little salt and pepper. Brush a griddle pan with the oil, then heat on the stove until smoking hot.

2 Place the duck skinned-side down in the pan. Cook over a medium-high heat for 5 minutes, or until well browned. Turn the duck and cook for 2 minutes. Lower the heat and cook for a further 5–8 minutes, or until cooked but still slightly pink in the centre. Remove from the pan and keep warm.

3 While the duck is cooking, make the sauce. Put the orange juice, bay leaf, redcurrant jelly, fresh or frozen and dried berries and sugar in a small saucepan. Add any juices left in the griddle pan to the small pan. Slowly bring to the boil, lower the heat and simmer uncovered for 4–5 minutes, until the fruit is soft.

4 Remove the bay leaf. Stir in the vinegar and chopped mint and season to taste with salt and pepper.

5 Slice the duck breasts on the diagonal and arrange on serving plates. Spoon over the berry sauce and garnish with sprigs of fresh mint. Serve immediately with the potatoes and green beans.

Ingredients   SERVES 4

4 x 175 g/6 oz boneless duck breasts
salt and freshly ground black pepper
1 tsp sunflower oil

For the sauce:

juice of 1 orange
1 bay leaf
3 tbsp redcurrant jelly
150 g/5 oz fresh or frozen
    mixed berries
2 tbsp dried cranberries or cherries
$^1/_2$ tsp soft light brown sugar
1 tbsp balsamic vinegar
1 tsp freshly chopped mint
sprigs of fresh mint, to garnish

To serve:

freshly cooked potatoes
freshly cooked green beans

Helpful hint

Duck breasts are best served slightly pink in the middle. Whole ducks, however, should be thoroughly cooked.

Rabbit Italian

1   Trim the rabbit if necessary. Chop the bacon and reserve.
    Chop the garlic and onion and slice the carrot thinly, then
    trim the celery and chop.

2   Heat the butter and 1 tablespoon of the oil in a large
    saucepan and brown the rabbit for 5 minutes, stirring
    frequently, until sealed all over. Transfer the rabbit to a plate
    and reserve.

3   Add the garlic, bacon, celery, carrot and onion to the
    saucepan and cook for a further 5 minutes, stirring
    occasionally, until softened, then return the rabbit to the
    saucepan and pour over the tomatoes with their juice and
    the wine. Season to taste with salt and pepper. Bring to the
    boil, cover, reduce the heat and simmer for 45 minutes.

4   Meanwhile, wipe the mushrooms and, if large, cut in half.
    Heat the remaining oil in a small frying pan and sauté the
    mushrooms for 2 minutes. Drain, then add to the rabbit and
    cook for 15 minutes, or until the rabbit is tender. Season to
    taste and serve immediately with freshly cooked pasta and a
    green salad.

Ingredients   SERVES 4

450 g/1 lb diced rabbit,
   thawed if frozen
6 rashers streaky bacon
1 garlic clove, peeled
1 onion, peeled
1 carrot, peeled
1 celery stalk
25 g/1 oz butter
2 tbsp olive oil
400 g can chopped tomatoes
150 ml/$^1/_4$ pint red wine
salt and freshly ground black pepper
125 g/4 oz mushrooms

To serve:

freshly cooked pasta
green salad

Helpful hint

If you prefer to buy a whole rabbit,
have your butcher joint it for you into
8 pieces. The method and cooking
time will remain the same.

Traditional Lasagne

1 Preheat the oven to 200°C/400°F/Gas Mark 6, 15 minutes before cooking. Cook the beef and pancetta in a large saucepan for 10 minutes, stirring to break up any lumps. Add the onion, celery and mushrooms and cook for 4 minutes, or until softened slightly.

2 Stir in the garlic and 1 tablespoon of the flour, then cook for 1 minute. Stir in the stock, herbs and tomato purée. Season to taste with salt and pepper. Bring to the boil, then cover, reduce the heat and simmer for 45 minutes.

3 Meanwhile, melt the butter in a small saucepan and stir in the remaining flour, mustard powder and nutmeg, until well blended. Cook for 2 minutes. Remove from the heat and gradually blend in the milk until smooth. Return to the heat and bring to the boil, stirring, until thickened. Gradually stir in half the Parmesan and Cheddar cheeses until melted. Season to taste.

4 Spoon half the meat mixture into the base of a large ovenproof dish. Top with a single layer of pasta. Spread over half the sauce and scatter with half the cheese. Repeat the layers, finishing with cheese. Bake in the preheated oven for 30 minutes, or until the pasta is cooked and the top is golden brown and bubbly. Serve immediately with crusty bread and a green salad.

Ingredients   SERVES 4

450 g/1 lb lean minced beef steak
175 g/6 oz pancetta or smoked
   streaky bacon, chopped
1 large onion, peeled and chopped
2 celery stalks, trimmed and chopped
125 g/4 oz button mushrooms,
   wiped and chopped
2 garlic cloves, peeled and chopped
90 g/3$\frac{1}{2}$ oz plain flour
300 ml/$\frac{1}{2}$ pint beef stock
1 tbsp freeze-dried mixed herbs
5 tbsp tomato purée
salt and freshly ground black pepper
75 g/3 oz butter
1 tsp English mustard powder
pinch of freshly grated nutmeg
900 ml/1$\frac{1}{2}$ pints milk
125 g/4 oz Parmesan cheese, grated
125 g/4 oz Cheddar cheese, grated
8–12 precooked lasagne sheets

To serve:
crusty bread
fresh green salad leaves

Pan-fried Beef with Creamy Mushrooms

1 Cut the shallots in half if large, then chop the garlic. Heat the oil in a large frying pan and cook the shallots for about 8 minutes, stirring occasionally, until almost softened. Add the garlic and beef and cook for 8–10 minutes, turning once during cooking, until the meat is browned all over. Using a slotted spoon, transfer the beef to a plate and keep warm.

2 Rinse the tomatoes and cut into eighths, then wipe and slice the mushrooms. Add to the pan and cook for 5 minutes, stirring frequently, until the mushrooms have softened.

3 Pour in the brandy and heat through. Draw the pan off the heat and carefully ignite. Allow the flames to subside. Pour in the wine, return to the heat and bring to the boil. Boil until reduced by one third. Draw the pan off the heat, season to taste with salt and pepper, add the cream and stir.

4 Arrange the beef on serving plates and spoon over the sauce. Serve with baby new potatoes and a few green beans.

Ingredients SERVES 4

225 g/8 oz shallots, peeled
2 garlic cloves, peeled
2 tbsp olive oil
4 medallions of beef
4 plum tomatoes
125 g/4 oz flat mushrooms
3 tbsp brandy
150 ml/$^1/_4$ pint red wine
salt and freshly ground black pepper
4 tbsp double cream

To serve:
baby new potatoes
freshly cooked green beans

Helpful hint
To prepare medallions of beef, buy a piece of fillet weighing approximately 700 g/1$^1/_2$ lb. Cut crosswise into 4 pieces.

Fillet Steaks with Tomato & Garlic Sauce

1 Make a small cross on the top of each tomato and place in a large bowl. Cover with boiling water and leave for 2 minutes. Using a slotted spoon, remove the tomatoes and skin carefully. Repeat until all the tomatoes are skinned. Place on a chopping board, cut into quarters, remove the seeds and chop roughly, then reserve.

2 Peel and chop the garlic. Heat half the olive oil in a saucepan and cook the garlic for 30 seconds. Add the chopped tomatoes with the basil, oregano and red wine and season to taste with salt and pepper. Bring to the boil, then reduce the heat, cover and simmer for 15 minutes, stirring occasionally, or until the sauce is reduced and thickened. Stir the olives into the sauce and keep warm while cooking the steaks.

3 Meanwhile, lightly oil a griddle pan or heavy-based frying pan with the remaining olive oil and cook the steaks for 2 minutes on each side to seal. Continue to cook the steaks for a further 2–4 minutes, depending on personal preference. Serve the steaks immediately with the garlic sauce and freshly cooked vegetables.

Ingredients   SERVES 4

700 g/1½ lb ripe tomatoes
2 garlic cloves
2 tbsp olive oil
2 tbsp freshly chopped basil
2 tbsp freshly chopped oregano
2 tbsp red wine
salt and freshly ground black pepper
75 g/3 oz pitted black
    olives, chopped
4 fillet steaks, about 175 g/6 oz
    each in weight
freshly cooked vegetables, to serve

Helpful hint

Fillet steak should be a deep mahogany colour with a good marbling of fat. If the meat is bright red or if the fat is bright white the meat has not been aged properly and will probably be quite tough.

1

2

3

Chinese Beef with Angel Hair Pasta

1 Crush the peppercorns using a pestle and mortar. Transfer to a shallow bowl and combine with the chilli powder, Szechuan pepper, light soy sauce and sherry. Add the beef strips and stir until lightly coated. Cover and place in the refrigerator to marinate for 3 hours; stir occasionally during this time.

2 When ready to cook, bring a large pan of lightly salted water to a rolling boil. Add the pasta and cook according to the packet instructions, or until 'al dente'. Drain thoroughly and return to the pan. Add the sesame oil and toss lightly. Keep the pasta warm.

3 Heat a wok or large frying pan, add the sunflower oil and heat until very hot. Add the shredded spring onions with the sliced red and green peppers and stir-fry for 2 minutes.

4 Drain the beef, reserving the marinade, then add the beef to the wok or pan and stir-fry for 3 minutes. Pour in the marinade and stir-fry for 1–2 minutes, until the steak is tender.

5 Pile the pasta onto 4 warmed plates. Top with the stir-fried beef and peppers and garnish with toasted sesame seeds and shredded spring onions. Serve immediately.

Ingredients   SERVES 4

1 tbsp pink peppercorns
1 tbsp chilli powder
1 tbsp Szechuan pepper
3 tbsp light soy sauce
3 tbsp dry sherry
450 g/1 lb sirloin steak, cut into strips
350 g/12 oz angel hair pasta
1 tbsp sesame oil
1 tbsp sunflower oil
1 bunch spring onions, trimmed and finely shredded, plus extra to garnish
1 red pepper, deseeded and thinly sliced
1 green pepper, deseeded and thinly sliced
1 tbsp toasted sesame seeds, to garnish

Food fact

Szechuan pepper is the reddish-brown dried berry of the Chinese prickly ash tree and has a pronounced spicy, woody flavour. It is one of the essential ingredients of Chinese five-spice powder.

Lamb Meatballs with Savoy Cabbage

1 Place the lamb mince in a large bowl with the parsley, ginger, light soy sauce and egg yolk and mix together. Divide the mixture into walnut-size pieces and, using your hands, roll into balls. Place on a baking sheet, cover with clingfilm and chill in the refrigerator for at least 30 minutes.

2 Meanwhile, blend together the dark soy sauce, sherry and cornflour with 2 tablespoons of water in a small bowl until smooth. Reserve.

3 Heat a wok, add the oil and when hot, add the meatballs and cook for 5–8 minutes, or until browned all over, turning occasionally. Using a slotted spoon, transfer the meatballs to a large plate and keep warm.

4 Add the garlic, spring onions, Savoy cabbage and the Chinese leaves to the wok and stir-fry for 3 minutes. Pour over the reserved soy sauce mixture, bring to the boil, then simmer for 30 seconds or until thickened. Return the meatballs to the wok and mix in. Garnish with chopped red chilli and serve immediately.

As the ingredients include raw egg, make sure the meatballs are cooked thoroughly.

Ingredients   SERVES 4

450 g/1 lb fresh lamb mince
1 tbsp freshly chopped parsley
1 tbsp freshly grated root ginger
1 tbsp light soy sauce
1 medium egg yolk
4 tbsp dark soy sauce
2 tbsp dry sherry
1 tbsp cornflour
3 tbsp vegetable oil
2 garlic cloves, peeled and chopped
1 bunch spring onions, trimmed
  and shredded
$^1/_2$ Savoy cabbage, trimmed
  and shredded
$^1/_2$ head Chinese leaves, trimmed
  and shredded
freshly chopped red chilli, to garnish

Tasty tip

This dish is made with basic ingredients, but you can substitute more Chinese ingredients if you prefer, such as rice wine vinegar instead of sherry and pak choi leaves instead of Savoy cabbage.

Roasted Lamb with Rosemary & Garlic

1 Preheat the oven to 200°C/400°F/Gas Mark 6, 15 minutes before roasting. Wipe the leg of lamb with a clean, damp cloth, then place the lamb in a large roasting tin. With a sharp knife, make small, deep incisions into the meat. Cut 2–3 garlic cloves into small slivers, then insert with a few small sprigs of rosemary into the lamb. Season to taste with salt and pepper and cover the lamb with the slices of pancetta.

2 Drizzle over 1 tablespoon of the olive oil and lay a few more rosemary sprigs across the lamb. Roast in the preheated oven for 30 minutes, then pour over the vinegar.

3 Peel the potatoes and cut into large dice. Peel the onion and cut into thick wedges, then thickly slice the remaining garlic. Arrange around the lamb. Pour the remaining olive oil over the potatoes, then reduce the oven temperature to 180°C/350°F/Gas Mark 4 and roast for a further 1 hour, or until the lamb is tender. Garnish with fresh sprigs of rosemary and serve immediately with the roast potatoes and ratatouille.

Ingredients   SERVES 6

1.6 kg/3¹/₂ lb leg of lamb
8 garlic cloves, peeled
few sprigs of fresh rosemary
salt and freshly ground black pepper
4 slices pancetta
4 tbsp olive oil
4 tbsp red wine vinegar
900 g/2 lb potatoes
1 large onion
sprigs of fresh rosemary, to garnish
freshly cooked ratatouille, to serve

Helpful hint

If you are unable to get a leg of lamb weighing exactly 1.6 kg/3¹/₂ lb, calculate the cooking time as follows: 20 minutes per 450 g/1 lb plus 30 minutes for rare, 25 minutes per 450 g/1 lb plus 30 minutes for medium and 30 minutes per 450 g/1 lb plus 30 minutes for well done.

Marinated Lamb Chops with Garlic-fried Potatoes

1 Trim the chops of any excess fat, wipe with a clean damp cloth and reserve. To make the marinade, using a pestle and mortar, pound the thyme leaves and rosemary with the salt until pulpy. Add the garlic and continue pounding until crushed. Stir in the lemon rind and juice and the olive oil.

2 Pour the marinade over the lamb chops, turning them until they are well coated. Cover lightly and leave to marinate in the refrigerator for about 1 hour.

3 Meanwhile, heat the oil in a large non-stick frying pan. Add the potatoes and garlic and cook over a low heat for about 20 minutes, stirring occasionally. Increase the heat and cook for a further 10–15 minutes until golden. Drain on absorbent kitchen paper and add salt to taste. Keep warm.

4 Heat a griddle pan until almost smoking. Add the lamb chops and cook for 3–4 minutes on each side until golden, but still pink in the middle. Serve with the potatoes and either a mixed salad or freshly cooked vegetables.

Ingredients   SERVES 4

4 thick lamb chops

For the marinade:
1 small bunch fresh thyme,
    leaves removed
1 tbsp freshly chopped rosemary
1 tsp salt
2 garlic cloves, peeled and crushed
rind and juice of 1 lemon
2 tbsp olive oil

For the garlic-fried potatoes:
3 tbsp olive oil
550 g/1¼ lb potatoes, peeled and
    cut into 1 cm/½ inch dice
6 unpeeled garlic cloves

mixed salad or freshly cooked
    vegetables, to serve

Tasty tip
Try other citrus juices in this recipe for a change (the acids also help to tenderise).

Lamb Pilaf

1 Preheat the oven to 140°C/275°F/Gas Mark 1. Heat the oil in a flameproof casserole with a tight-fitting lid and add the almonds. Cook for about 1 minute until just starting to brown, stirring often. Add the onion, carrot and celery and cook gently for a further 8–10 minutes until soft and lightly browned.

2 Increase the heat and add the lamb. Cook for a further 5 minutes until the lamb has changed colour. Add the ground cinnamon and chilli flakes and stir briefly before adding the tomatoes and orange rind.

3 Stir and add the rice, then the stock. Bring slowly to the boil and cover tightly. Transfer to the preheated oven and cook for 30–35 minutes until the rice is tender and the stock is absorbed.

4 Remove from the oven and leave to stand for 5 minutes before stirring in the chives and coriander. Season to taste with salt and pepper. Garnish with the lemon slices and sprigs of fresh coriander and serve immediately.

Ingredients   SERVES 4

2 tbsp vegetable oil
25 g/1 oz flaked or slivered almonds
1 medium onion, peeled and
   finely chopped
1 medium carrot, peeled and
   finely chopped
1 celery stalk, trimmed and
   finely chopped
350 g/12 oz lean lamb, cut into chunks
$\frac{1}{4}$ tsp ground cinnamon
$\frac{1}{4}$ tsp chilli flakes
2 large tomatoes, skinned, deseeded
   and chopped
grated rind of 1 orange
350 g/12 oz easy-cook brown
   basmati rice
600 ml/1 pint vegetable or lamb stock
2 tbsp freshly snipped chives
3 tbsp freshly chopped coriander
salt and freshly ground black pepper

To garnish:
lemon slices
sprigs of fresh coriander

Sweet-&-Sour Spareribs

1 Preheat the oven to 200°C/400°F/Gas Mark 6, 15 minutes before cooking. If necessary, place the ribs on a chopping board and, using a sharp knife, cut the joint in between the ribs, to form single ribs. Place the ribs in a shallow dish in a single layer.

2 Spoon the honey, Worcestershire sauce, Chinese five-spice powder, soy sauce, sherry and chilli sauce into a small saucepan and heat gently, stirring until smooth. Stir in the chopped garlic, tomato purée and mustard powder, if using.

3 Pour the honey mixture over the ribs and spoon over until the ribs are coated evenly. Cover with clingfilm and leave to marinate overnight in the refrigerator, occasionally spooning the marinade over the ribs.

4 When ready to cook, remove the ribs from the marinade and place in a shallow roasting tin. Spoon over a little of the marinade and reserve the remainder. Place the spareribs in the preheated oven and cook for 35–40 minutes, or until cooked and the outsides are crisp. Baste occasionally with the reserved marinade during cooking. Garnish with a few spring onion curls and serve immediately, either as a starter or as a meat accompaniment.

Ingredients   SERVES 4

1.6 kg/3$^1/_2$ lb pork spareribs
4 tbsp clear honey
1 tbsp Worcestershire sauce
1 tsp Chinese five-spice powder
4 tbsp soy sauce
2$^1/_2$ tbsp dry sherry
1 tsp chilli sauce
2 garlic cloves, peeled and chopped
1$^1/_2$ tbsp tomato purée
1 tsp dry mustard powder (optional)
spring onion curls, to garnish

Handy hint

Marinating spareribs overnight not only flavours the meat, but makes it wonderfully tender as well. If you do not have enough time for this, place the ribs in a saucepan and pour in enough water to just cover. Add 1 tablespoon of wine vinegar, bring to the boil, then simmer gently for 15 minutes. Drain well, toss in the marinade and roast straight away, basting occasionally as before.

Antipasto Penne

1 Preheat the grill just before cooking. Cut the courgettes into thick slices. Rinse the tomatoes and cut into quarters, then cut the ham into strips. Pour the oil into a baking dish and place under the grill for 2 minutes, or until almost smoking. Remove from the grill and stir in the courgettes. Return to the grill and cook for 8 minutes, stirring occasionally. Remove from the grill and add the tomatoes and cook for a further 3 minutes.

2 Add the ham to the baking dish and cook under the grill for 4 minutes, until all the vegetables are charred and the ham is brown. Season to taste with salt and pepper.

3 Meanwhile, plunge the pasta into a large saucepan of lightly salted boiling water, return to a rolling boil, stir and cook for 8 minutes, or until 'al dente'. Drain well and return to the saucepan.

4 Stir the antipasto into the vegetables and cook under the grill for 2 minutes, or until heated through. Add the cooked pasta and toss together gently with the remaining ingredients. Grill for a further 4 minutes, then serve immediately.

Ingredients   SERVES 4

3 medium courgettes, trimmed
4 plum tomatoes
175 g/6 oz Italian ham
2 tbsp olive oil
salt and freshly ground black pepper
350 g/12 oz dried penne pasta
285 g jar antipasto
125 g/4 oz mozzarella cheese, drained and diced
125 g/4 oz Gorgonzola cheese, crumbled
3 tbsp freshly chopped flat-leaf parsley

Food fact

The term antipasto refers to the course served before the pasto or meal begins and its purpose is to whet the appetite for the following courses. In Italy, these are served in small quantities, though 2 or 3 different dishes may be served at once. There are no hard and fast rules as to what constitutes a suitable dish for antipasti – there are literally thousands of regional variations.

Jamaican Jerk Pork with Rice & Beans

1 To make the jerk pork marinade, purée the onions, garlic, lime juice, molasses, soy sauce, ginger, chillies, cinnamon, allspice and nutmeg together in a food processor until smooth. Put the pork chops into a plastic or non-reactive dish and pour over the marinade, turning the chops to coat. Marinate in the refrigerator for at least 1 hour or overnight.

2 Drain the beans and place in a large saucepan with about 2 litres/3¹/₂ pints cold water. Bring to the boil and boil rapidly for 10 minutes. Reduce the heat, cover and simmer gently for 1 hour until tender, adding more water, if necessary. When cooked, drain well and mash roughly.

3 Heat the oil for the rice in a saucepan with a tight-fitting lid and add the onion, celery and garlic. Cook gently for 5 minutes until softened. Add the bay leaves, rice and stock and stir. Bring to the boil, cover and cook very gently for 10 minutes. Add the beans and stir well again. Cook for a further 5 minutes, then remove from the heat. Remove the bay leaves.

4 Heat a griddle pan until almost smoking. Remove the pork chops from the marinade, scraping off any surplus and add to the hot pan. Cook for 5–8 minutes on each side, or until cooked. Garnish with the parsley and serve immediately with the rice.

Ingredients   SERVES 4

175 g/6 oz dried red kidney beans,
    soaked overnight
2 onions, peeled and chopped
2 garlic cloves, peeled and crushed
4 tbsp lime juice
2 tbsp each dark molasses, soy sauce
    and chopped fresh root ginger
2 jalapeño chillies, deseeded
    and chopped
¹/₂ tsp ground cinnamon
¹/₄ tsp each ground allspice and
    ground nutmeg
4 pork loin chops, on the bone

For the rice:

1 tbsp vegetable oil
1 onion, peeled and finely chopped
1 celery stalk, trimmed and finely sliced
3 garlic cloves, peeled and crushed
2 bay leaves
225 g/8 oz long-grain white rice
475 ml/18 fl oz chicken or ham stock
sprigs of fresh flat-leaf parsley,
    to garnish

Pork Chop Hotpot

1 Preheat the oven to 190°C/375°F/Gas Mark 5, 10 minutes before cooking. Trim the pork chops, removing any excess fat, wipe with a clean, damp cloth, then dust with a little flour and reserve. Cut the shallots in half if large. Chop the garlic and slice the sun-dried tomatoes.

2 Heat the olive oil in a large casserole and cook the pork chops for about 5 minutes, turning occasionally during cooking, until browned all over. Using a slotted spoon, carefully lift out of the dish and reserve. Add the shallots and cook for 5 minutes, stirring occasionally.

3 Return the pork chops to the casserole and scatter with the garlic and sun-dried tomatoes, then pour over the can of tomatoes with their juice.

4 Blend the red wine, stock and tomato purée together and add the chopped oregano. Season to taste with salt and pepper, then pour over the pork chops and bring to a gentle boil. Cover with a close-fitting lid and cook in the preheated oven for 1 hour, or until the pork chops are tender. Adjust the seasoning to taste, then scatter with a few oregano leaves and serve immediately with freshly cooked potatoes and French beans.

Ingredients   SERVES 4

4 pork chops
flour for dusting
225 g/8 oz shallots, peeled
2 garlic cloves, peeled
50 g/2 oz sun-dried tomatoes
2 tbsp olive oil
400 g can plum tomatoes
150 ml/¼ pint red wine
150 ml/¼ pint chicken stock
3 tbsp tomato purée
2 tbsp freshly chopped oregano
salt and freshly ground black pepper
fresh oregano leaves, to garnish

To serve:
freshly cooked new potatoes
French beans

Tasty tip
Choose bone-in chops for this recipe. Remove any excess fat and rind before cooking.

Spiced Couscous & Vegetables

1   Heat the oil in a large frying pan and add the shallot and garlic and cook for 2–3 minutes until softened. Add the peppers and aubergine and reduce the heat.

2   Cook for 8–10 minutes until the vegetables are tender, adding a little water if necessary.

3   Test a piece of aubergine to ensure it is cooked through. Add all the spices and cook for a further minute, stirring.

4   Increase the heat and add the tomatoes and lemon juice. Cook for 2–3 minutes until the tomatoes have started to break down. Remove from the heat and leave to cool slightly.

5   Meanwhile, put the couscous into a large bowl. Bring the stock to the boil in a saucepan, then pour over the couscous. Stir well and cover with a clean tea towel.

6   Leave to stand for 7–8 minutes until all the stock is absorbed and the couscous is tender.

7   Uncover the couscous and fluff with a fork. Stir in the vegetable and spice mixture along with the raisins, almonds, parsley and coriander. Season to taste with salt and pepper and serve.

Ingredients   SERVES 4

1 tbsp olive oil
1 large shallot, peeled and
   finely chopped
1 garlic clove, peeled and
   finely chopped
1 small red pepper, deseeded
   and cut into strips
1 small yellow pepper, deseeded
   and cut into strips
1 small aubergine, diced
1 tsp each turmeric, ground cumin,
   ground cinnamon and paprika
2 tsp ground coriander
large pinch saffron strands
2 tomatoes, peeled, deseeded
   and diced
2 tbsp lemon juice
225 g/8 oz couscous
225 ml/8 fl oz vegetable stock
2 tbsp raisins
2 tbsp whole almonds
2 tbsp freshly chopped parsley
2 tbsp freshly chopped coriander
salt and freshly ground black pepper

Chinese Salad with Soy & Ginger Dressing

1 Rinse and finely shred the Chinese cabbage and place in a serving dish.

2 Slice the water chestnuts into small slivers and cut the spring onions diagonally into 2.5 cm/1 inch lengths, then split lengthways into thin strips.

3 Cut the tomatoes in half and then slice each half into 3 wedges and reserve.

4 Simmer the mangetout in boiling water for 2 minutes until beginning to soften, drain and cut in half diagonally.

5 Arrange the water chestnuts, spring onions, mangetout, tomatoes and bean sprouts on top of the shredded Chinese cabbage. Garnish with the freshly chopped coriander.

6 Make the dressing by whisking all the ingredients together in a small bowl until thoroughly mixed. Serve with the bread and the salad.

Ingredients   SERVES 4

1 head of Chinese cabbage
200 g can water chestnuts, drained
6 spring onions, trimmed
4 ripe but firm cherry tomatoes
125 g/4 oz mangetout
125 g/4 oz bean sprouts
2 tbsp freshly chopped coriander

For the soy and ginger dressing:

2 tbsp sunflower oil
4 tbsp light soy sauce
2.5 cm/1 inch piece root ginger,
    peeled and finely grated
zest and juice of 1 lemon
salt and freshly ground black pepper
crusty white bread, to serve

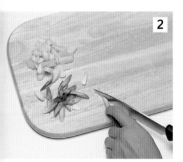

Marinated Vegetable Kebabs

1   Place the courgettes, peppers and baby onions in a pan of just-boiled water. Bring back to the boil and simmer for about 30 seconds.

2   Drain and rinse the cooked vegetables in cold water and dry on absorbent kitchen paper.

3   Thread the cooked vegetables and the mushrooms and tomatoes alternately onto skewers and place in a large shallow dish.

4   Make the marinade by whisking all the ingredients together until thoroughly blended. Pour the marinade evenly over the kebabs, then chill in the refrigerator for at least 1 hour. Spoon the marinade over the kebabs occasionally during this time.

5   Place the kebabs in a hot griddle pan or on a hot barbecue and cook gently for 10–12 minutes. Turn the kebabs frequently and brush with the marinade when needed. When the vegetables are tender, sprinkle over the chopped parsley and serve immediately with couscous.

Ingredients   SERVES 4

2 small courgettes, cut into
  2 cm/$^3/_4$ inch pieces
$^1/_2$ green pepper, deseeded and cut
  into 2.5 cm/1 inch pieces
$^1/_2$ red pepper, deseeded and cut
  into 2.5 cm/1 inch pieces
$^1/_2$ yellow pepper, deseeded and
  cut into 2.5 cm/1 inch pieces
8 baby onions, peeled
8 button mushrooms
8 cherry tomatoes
freshly chopped parsley, to garnish
freshly cooked couscous, to serve

For the marinade:

1 tbsp light olive oil
4 tbsp dry sherry
2 tbsp light soy sauce
1 red chilli, deseeded and
  finely chopped
2 garlic cloves, peeled and crushed
2.5 cm/1 inch piece root ginger,
  peeled and finely grated

Stuffed Tomatoes with Grilled Polenta

1 Preheat the grill just before cooking. To make the polenta, pour the stock into a saucepan. Add a pinch of salt and bring to the boil. Pour in the polenta in a fine stream, stirring all the time. Simmer for about 15 minutes, or until very thick. Stir in the butter and add a little pepper. Turn the polenta out onto a chopping board and spread to a thickness of just over 1 cm/^{1}/$_2$ inch. Cool, cover with clingfilm and chill in the refrigerator for 30 minutes.

2 To make the stuffed tomatoes, cut the tomatoes in half, then scoop out the seeds and press through a fine sieve to extract the juices. Season the insides of the tomatoes with salt and pepper and reserve. Heat the olive oil in a saucepan and gently fry the garlic and spring onions for 3 minutes. Add the tomatoes' juices, bubble for 3–4 minutes, until most of the liquid has evaporated. Stir in the herbs, Parma ham and a little black pepper with half the breadcrumbs. Spoon into the hollowed-out tomatoes and reserve.

3 Cut the polenta into 5 cm/2 inch squares, then cut each in half to make triangles. Put the triangles onto a piece of foil on the grill rack and grill for 4–5 minutes on each side until golden. Cover and keep warm. Grill the tomatoes under a medium-hot grill for about 4 minutes – any exposed Parma ham will become crisp. Sprinkle with the remaining breadcrumbs and grill for 1–2 minutes, or until golden brown. Garnish with snipped chives and serve immediately with the grilled polenta.

Ingredients   SERVES 4

For the polenta:

300 ml/^{1}/$_2$ pint vegetable stock
salt and freshly ground black pepper
50 g/2 oz quick-cook polenta
15 g/^{1}/$_2$ oz butter

For the stuffed tomatoes:

4 large tomatoes
1 tbsp olive oil
1 garlic clove, peeled and crushed
1 bunch spring onions, trimmed and
   finely chopped
2 tbsp freshly chopped parsley
2 tbsp freshly chopped basil
2 slices Parma ham, cut into
   thin slivers
50 g/2 oz fresh white breadcrumbs
snipped chives, to garnish

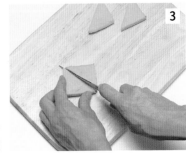

Three-tomato Pizzas

1 Preheat the oven to 220°C/425°F/Gas Mark 7. Place a baking sheet into the oven to heat up.

2 Divide the prepared pizza dough into 4 equal pieces. Roll out one quarter of the pizza dough onto a lightly floured board to form a 20.5 cm/8 inch round. Lightly cover the 3 remaining pieces of dough with clingfilm.

3 Roll out the other 3 pieces into rounds, one at a time. While rolling out any piece of dough, keep the others covered with the clingfilm.

4 Slice the plum tomatoes, halve the cherry tomatoes and chop the sun-dried tomatoes into small pieces.

5 Place a few pieces of each type of tomato onto each pizza base then season to taste with the sea salt.

6 Sprinkle with the chopped basil and drizzle with the olive oil. Place a few slices of mozzarella on each pizza and season with black pepper.

7 Transfer the pizzas onto the heated baking sheet and cook for 15–20 minutes, or until the cheese is golden brown and bubbling. Garnish with the basil leaves and serve immediately.

Ingredients   SERVES 2–4

1 quantity pizza dough
3 plum tomatoes
8 cherry tomatoes
6 sun-dried tomatoes
pinch of sea salt
1 tbsp freshly chopped basil
2 tbsp extra virgin olive oil
125 g/4 oz buffalo mozzarella
  cheese, sliced
freshly ground black pepper
fresh basil leaves, to garnish

Food fact

Buffalo mozzarella is considered the king of mozzarellas. It uses buffalo milk, which results in the cheese tasting extremely mild and creamy. A good mozzarella should come in liquid to keep it moist and should tear easily into chunks.

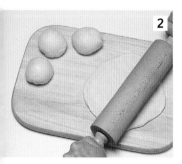

Smoked Mackerel Vol-au-Vents

1 Preheat the oven to 230°C/450°F/Gas Mark 8. Roll the pastry out on a lightly floured surface and, using a 9 cm/3½ inch fluted cutter, cut out 12 rounds.

2 Using a 1 cm/½ inch cutter, mark a lid in the centre of each round.

3 Place on a damp baking sheet and brush the rounds with a little beaten egg.

4 Sprinkle the pastry with the sesame seeds and bake in the preheated oven for 10–12 minutes, or until golden brown and well risen.

5 Transfer the vol-au-vents to a chopping board and, when cool enough to touch, carefully remove the lids with a small, sharp knife.

6 Scoop out any uncooked pastry from the inside of each vol-au-vent, then return to the oven for 5–8 minutes to dry out. Remove and allow to cool.

7 Flake the mackerel into small pieces and reserve. Peel the cucumber if desired, cut into very small dice and add to the mackerel.

8 Beat the soft cream cheese with the cranberry sauce, dill and lemon rind. Stir in the mackerel and cucumber and use to fill the vol-au-vents. Place the lids on top and garnish with dill sprigs.

Ingredients   MAKES 12

350 g/12 oz prepared puff pastry
1 small egg, beaten
2 tsp sesame seeds
225 g/8 oz peppered smoked
    mackerel, skinned and chopped
5 cm/2 inch piece cucumber
4 tbsp soft cream cheese
2 tbsp cranberry sauce
1 tbsp freshly chopped dill
1 tbsp finely grated lemon rind
dill sprigs, to garnish
mixed salad leaves, to serve

Food fact

Mackerel is a relatively cheap fish and one of the richest sources of minerals, oils and vitamins available. This dish is an affordable way to incorporate all these essential nutrients into your diet.

1

5

8

Seared Pancetta-wrapped Cod

1 Wipe the cod fillets and wrap each one with the pancetta. Secure each fillet with a cocktail stick and reserve.

2 Drain the capers and soak in cold water for 10 minutes to remove any excess vinegar, then drain and reserve.

3 Heat the oil in a large frying pan and sear the wrapped pieces of cod fillet for about 3 minutes on each side, turning carefully with a fish slice so as not to break up the fish.

4 Lower the heat then continue to cook for 2–3 minutes or until the fish is cooked thoroughly.

5 Meanwhile, place the reserved capers, lemon juice and olive oil into a small saucepan. Grind over the black pepper.

6 Place the saucepan over a low heat and bring to a gentle simmer, stirring continuously, for 2–3 minutes.

7 Once the fish is cooked, garnish with the parsley and serve with the warm caper dressing, freshly cooked vegetables and new potatoes.

Ingredients   SERVES 4

4 x 175 g/6 oz thick cod fillets
4 very thin slices of pancetta
3 tbsp capers in vinegar
1 tbsp vegetable or sunflower oil
2 tbsp lemon juice
1 tbsp olive oil
freshly ground black pepper
1 tbsp freshly chopped parsley,
    to garnish

To serve:

freshly cooked vegetables
new potatoes

Food fact

Pancetta is Italian-cured belly pork, which is often delicately smoked and sold either finely sliced or chopped roughly into small cubes. The slices of pancetta can be used to encase poultry and fish, whereas chopped pancetta is often used in sauces. To cook chopped pancetta, fry for 2–3 minutes and reserve. Use the oil to seal meat or to fry onions, then return the pancetta to the pan.

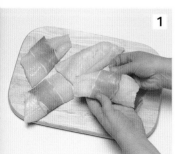

1

3

6

Sticky-glazed Spatchcocked Poussins

1 Preheat the grill just before cooking. Place one of the poussins breast-side down on a board. Using poultry shears, cut down one side of the backbone. Cut down the other side of the backbone. Remove the bone. Open out the poussin and press down hard on the breast bone with the heel of your hand to break it and to flatten the poussin.

2 Thread two skewers crosswise through the bird to keep it flat, ensuring that each skewer goes through a wing and out through the leg on the opposite side. Repeat with the other bird. Season both sides of the bird with salt and pepper.

3 To make the glaze, mix together the lemon zest and juice, sherry, honey, soy sauce, mustard, tomato purée and Chinese five-spice powder and use to brush all over the poussins.

4 Place the poussins skin-side down on a grill rack and grill under a medium heat for 15 minutes, brushing halfway through with more glaze. Turn the poussins over and grill for 10 minutes. Brush again with glaze and arrange the kumquat slices on top. Grill for a further 15 minutes until well browned and cooked through. If they start to brown too quickly, turn down the grill a little.

5 Remove the skewers and cut each poussin in half along the breastbone. Serve immediately with the salad, bread or potatoes.

Ingredients   SERVES 4

2 poussins, each about 700 g/1 1/2 lb
salt and freshly ground black pepper
4 kumquats, thinly sliced
assorted salad leaves, crusty bread or
    new potatoes, to serve

For the glaze:

zest of 1 small lemon, finely grated
1 tbsp lemon juice
1 tbsp dry sherry
2 tbsp clear honey
2 tbsp dark soy sauce
2 tbsp wholegrain mustard
1 tsp tomato purée
1/2 tsp Chinese five-spice powder

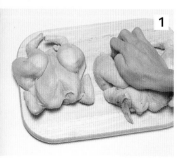

Index